MW01169067

PRAISE FOR THE BOOK

"I've known Ben and his family for over 20 years, and this book is a raw, gripping reflection of his personal journey. It serves as a reminder that even our finest leaders must deal with personal issues and that we all struggle each and every day. *God Was Always Speaking* is a must-read for anyone who has ever struggled, doubted their path, or sought a deeper sense of purpose."

Admiral Chris "Lung" Aquilino, USN (Ret)
26th Commander, US INDOPACIFIC Command

"This book was a revelation to me, and Ben's story will open your eyes and change your life. God is definitely good, and Ben is a beautiful example of how He works in our lives."

Bob Nied
PGA Teacher of the Year, North Texas PGA HOPE Lead Instructor

---

"Ben's story reminded me of the many times I have reflected back across my own life and realized that in all circumstances, God was right there with me, directing my steps regardless of my plans. Although Ben's journey and pain are real, if this book helps just one person see and become awed by God in the moment, rather than in hindsight, it will be worth every struggle he endured."

Captain Valerie Overstreet, USN (Ret)
First female to be selected as an E-2C squadron Commanding Officer and Commander, Airborne Command, Control and Logistics Wing

"A deeply moving and inspiring story that hits that spot right in your soul. No matter how complicated life may seem, you are never alone, and you are always a part of God's beautiful, unfolding plan."

Pastor Robert Garcia
US Army Ranger, President of Robert Garcia Agency

"Life's all about choices. Some we make consciously, others not. Then we wonder why we took the path we chose. 'It just happened,' and 'something made me take that road,' aren't always satisfying explanations of how and why we made significant life-changing decisions. Like the choices, some of the decisions we made were good, some bad —but they taught valuable lessons. *God Was Always Speaking, I Just Wasn't Listening* is the story of one man's journey through life until he had an epiphany that provided THE answer."

Marc Liebman
Retired Navy captain, Naval Aviator, and award-winning author.

"Heartfelt, funny, raw, and inspiring. It's an amazing story of hope. A Naval Officer's remarkable discovery of how God works with each of us through our hidden pain and brokenness, always leading us toward Christ where true healing can begin."

Peter Overland
Award-winning Creative Director and Marketing Executive, Fox Broadcasting, INSP Network, Imagicomm Films.

"As a pastor of over 30 years, I have been in the front-row seat to see countless people's faith emerging and developing. Seeing Ben and his family's journey has been a true joy. I love how transparent Ben is in this book and how he shares his unique path to faith. This book will speak to you if you are a curious onlooker or a devoted follower."

Pastor Eddie Woods
Senior Pastor, City Point Church

"This is a powerful example of someone who had it all but was missing out on the most important aspect of life: the power of God and a life fulfilled. This is what it's all about."

Terry DeWitt, PhD, AT, EP-C
Professor, Department of Kinesiology, Ouachita Baptist University
COL (R) US Army Reserve, and Army Reserve Ambassador

"I usually write out my thoughts longhand, but after reading Ben's journey of finding God and taking His hand to guide him through soul-searching, I was compelled to type this straight from my heart.

Ben's inspiring story made me reflect deeply on my own life and the moments I may have overlooked along the way. Ben, thank you for opening my eyes again and bringing me back to the solid ground from which I can continue to grow with my family. This is an incredible read."

Rear Admiral Mark R. Milliken, USN (Retired)
former Deputy Assistant Secretary of the Navy,
Commanding Officer of the USS Independence

"Ben's book captures his journey from feeling alone, even when a co-pilot was in the cockpit with him, to now knowing God is with him all the time. He flew with a purpose, Ben now **lives** with a purpose, and you don't want to put the book down until you finish it."

Brad Kaufman
Senior Special Agent, ATF Special Response Teams (retired)
Former Dallas PD, and Founder/Owner of Bravo Kilo Advisors

"Ben Duelley doesn't just tell his story—he invites you to walk with him through the shadows and into the light. God Was Always Speaking is a testament to resilience, love, and the quiet but powerful work of faith in the hardest of times. It's a book that speaks to the soul."

Kyle Gabhart
Author of *The Canteen: Abandon Self-Sufficiency and Fully Rely on God,* and *Legends Don't Retire: And neither should you*

GOD WAS ALWAYS SPEAKING, I JUST WASN'T LISTENING

A VETERAN'S JOURNEY FROM SUPPRESSION TO SALVATION

BEN DUELLEY

Disclaimer: In some instances, the author has changed the names of individuals to maintain their anonymity.

Library of Congress Control Number: 2025903625

Published by: Penta Eagles, Allen, TX

Cover Design: Daniel Eyenegho

To contact the author: Ben.duelley.author@gmail.com

 Formatted with Vellum

To my wife, Eleanor, who has stood next to me every step of the way.

And to God, who has led us through every step.

CONTENTS

.

PREFACE

On September 20, 2023, around 2:15 pm, it was brought to my attention that a low vibrational entity had attached itself to my body.

If you Google "low vibrational entity," you won't find many reputable sources explaining what it means—unless you count Reddit as valid. And honestly, at the time, I had no idea what those words meant either, they just really freaked me out.

Throughout my life, I have been "successful." I was a high school and Division I college athlete. I graduated from the United States Naval Academy. I am a father to three wonderful children and have an amazing wife. I am a retired Naval Officer, reaching the rank of Captain after spending 24 years serving my country. And along the way I got to fly in some of the coolest jets and planes on the planet. I had planned out my life; it was going perfectly, and every achievement felt like the result of my hard work.

On the surface, I seemed to be doing quite well.

But inside, I felt broken. I was bitter, doubting myself and my abilities. I thought I was in control of everything in my life, yet I couldn't shake the grip of depression and anxiety.

I now understand that I was possessed.

I know…that sounds crazy, right? But I wasn't "possessed" in the Hollywood sense—no one was strapped to a bed, drenched in sweat, spewing obscenities in a deep, distorted voice. But, something dark had latched onto my soul, feeding me lies I didn't even recognize.

All I knew was that life felt unbearable. There were many days when I no longer wanted to be alive.

To put it bluntly, I had spent the previous nine months talking myself out of suicide.

And until September 20th, the day that I learned about this "low vibrational entity," I thought I was the one in charge of my life. I believed I was writing my own story.

But that all changed on September 21st. Because the day after I realized something dark had been feeding me lies, I found God. My life was about to take a positive turn, and I understood I was merely the pen He was using to write that story.

Since that day, the Lord has shown me that with Him and through Him, anything is possible. This journey in faith led me on a life-changing mission trip to El Salvador, where I saw miracles happen right before my eyes. I heard God's voice give me messages meant for strangers. And I even found myself face-to-face with a man battling his own demons.

Some of you reading this might think, "This dude is nuts."

That's okay. A year ago, I would've thought the same thing.

But I know that some of you have experienced similar struggles in your life, or are facing challenges right now. Maybe you too have felt the crushing sensation of anxiety overwhelming you, like an elephant sitting on your chest. Maybe you've laid down in a dark closet alone, sobbing uncontrollably for no reason whatsoever. Or maybe, you are just looking for some kind of meaning or purpose in your life. What-ever your circumstances, I hope this book opens a path for you to share your own experiences, both good and bad, just as it has for me.

And for someone out there, I know with absolute certainty that this book is meant for you. How do I know that, you ask?

Because on a sunny Thursday afternoon in September of 2023, I heard God's voice for the first time in my life, and He told me to tell this story—so He could place it in your hands.

This is not just my story. This is Our story.

PART ONE
BROKEN

Psalm 34:18 *"The Lord is close to the brokenhearted and saves those who are crushed in spirit."*

CHAPTER 1

KNOCKING ON HEAVEN'S DOOR

1 Peter 5:7 *"Give all your worries and cares to God, for he cares about you."*

Thursday, September 21, 2023. 9:05 AM

"Alrighty, y'all, let's start over," the man said in a calming, encouraging voice. "I'm Pastor Stephen, and like I mentioned, I'm the operations pastor here at City Point. What are your names again?"

Just 60 seconds earlier, my wife Eleanor and I had been strangers knocking on the back door of this very church outside of Dallas, Texas. After hours of searching for help online the night before, it felt as though God Himself had led me to City Point. No more writing things off as "weird coincidences"—this was divine intervention, plain and simple.

At exactly 9:00 AM, Eleanor stood next to me as I rang the doorbell at the church entrance, hoping—desperately—that someone who could help me would answer. Seeing no signs of life inside, we made our way to the back of the building, walking through the early morning dew that hadn't yet met the Texas heat. Cars were still parked across the street at the brewery where I had spent the previous night trying to ignore my problems.

Now, here we were, following Pastor Stephen through a maze of hallways into a cozy and tastefully furnished room. The walls were scattered with posters, and a coffee machine sat in the corner next to some white mugs and a bowl full of white Lifesavers. Through an open door, I could see long black curtains and stacks of digital equipment.

Was that the back of a stage? Why is there a stage here?

This place couldn't have been more different from the Lutheran church I attended as a kid.

Where were the stained-glass windows depicting The Last Supper? Shouldn't there be a big bell at the top that announces the hour?

"My name is Ben," I finally managed, taking a deep breath and trying to sound composed. "And this is Eleanor, my wife. And…"

I had already asked Pastor Stephen a seemingly insane question just a minute ago, and while he still invited us in, I couldn't shake the anxiety.

Though I had retired from the Navy a year earlier and hadn't flown in a Navy airplane for almost six years, it felt like I was back there all over again—sitting in an aircraft on the flight deck of an aircraft carrier, waiting for the catapult shot that launches your multimillion-dollar machine into the skies. There's a nervous energy mixed with fear that fills you in the seconds leading up to it. You know what's supposed to happen next, but there's always the chance that something could go wrong, and your guard is up. Way up. That's how I felt right then. My heart was pounding.

I had been to the emergency room so many times, only to be told I was fine. I'd seen counselors who either handed me pills or used their years of schooling to encourage me to just relax more, take a bath, or go for a walk. Here I was again, laying my soul bare to another human, this time with a story that made me sound like a crazy person. What if he didn't believe me either?

The air conditioner in the dimly lit room was on full blast, and drips of condensation fell from the ceiling, landing on the black leather sofa where my wife sat. Pastor Stephen was next to Eleanor on the other end of the sofa, waiting for me to continue. My wife hadn't said a word in over five minutes—not since she convinced me not to give up and go home. The room carried a distinct "church" aroma—reminiscent of walking into a Marriott lobby, with that clean, slightly luxurious blend of fresh linen and subtle citrus. But instead of calming me, it intensified the pounding in my head.

Remember those cartoons where a devil and an angel would stand on opposite shoulders, whispering competing words into the character's ears? This wasn't a cartoon, and I could hear the conflicting thoughts competing to drown each other out.

You know how crazy you sound, right? Just leave. Just say 'sorry, I made a mistake' and walk out the door.

One more deep breath in… long exhale out…

Suck it up, man. Get a hold of yourself. You can do this.

I repeated the question that had haunted me for the past 18 hours. "So, I've had some…things…happen to me recently. And I just need to know if the church believes—or if you believe—that a negative entity can attach itself to someone. And what do you do when that happens?"

Please believe me. Please believe me.

PART TWO
THE BEGINNING

John 1:1-4 "*In the beginning the Word already existed. The Word was with God, and the Word was God. He existed in the beginning with God. God created everything through him, and nothing was created except through him. The Word gave life to everything that was created, and his life brought light to everyone.*"

CHAPTER 2
FOUNDATIONS OF SUCCESS

Proverbs 16:9 *"We can make our plans, but the Lord determines our steps."*

I grew up in Tatamy, a small town in Pennsylvania, about 90 minutes north of Philadelphia. It was your typical Northeastern town where everyone knew each other, and most of our parents had gone to school together decades earlier. Life in Tatamy was simple, and family was everything.

Tatamy had just one 4-way flashing stoplight, mainly there to slow down traffic coming into Main Street from the neighboring town. And when I say Main Street, forget the quaint image of a picturesque town with mom-and-pop boutiques, cafes, and small-town businesses. We had a gas station on the west end and a tiny mini-mart six blocks to the east. Rolling fields separated the small towns that fed into our one high school in Nazareth, about three miles away.

Nazareth is famous for two things: Martin Guitar and being the home-town of Mario Andretti and his family. If you grew up there, odds were high that you knew someone who worked at Martin Guitar (like my dad), and you probably went trick-or-treating at the Andretti house, where he handed out his own personal Mario Andretti candy bars.

My parents, Cindy and Jeff, were high school sweethearts who raised me and my younger brother, Bryan, with a mix of love, unshakable support, and firm discipline. Like most kids who grew up before the turn of the century, we knew wooden spoons and belts weren't created just for their intended purposes. When my dad was angry, the message was clear: step up, take responsibility, and fix your mistakes. It wasn't always easy to swallow in the moment, but it laid the groundwork for the discipline and work ethic that have guided me ever since.

Even with those tough moments, my parents were unwavering in their support. They never missed a game, a match, or an event—from Little League to college. Whether I was on the mat, the field, or the stage, they were there, cheering me on. Their constant presence and high expectations taught me the value of persistence and accountability. I knew that if I worked hard enough, not only would I earn their pride, but I'd also live up to the standards they set for me—and, eventually, the standards I set for myself.

My grandparents lived just a few blocks away and were an integral part of my childhood. Nana and Pappy, my mom's parents, were a constant presence in our lives. Their house was close enough that we could stand in our front yard, look across the cornfield (unless it was October and the stalks were too high), and see if anyone was in their backyard using the pool. Sundays were family days, with my uncles, aunts, and cousins showing up at Nana and Pappy's house by mid-afternoon. Summers meant pool parties; winters meant backyard football.

Despite living in Philadelphia Eagles territory, Pappy somehow jumped ship and became a Cowboys fan in the 1960s, brainwashing a couple of his kids (my uncles), who in turn brainwashed their kids (my cousins). Those in the family who remained loyal to the home team were severely outnumbered on Sundays, and it was extra painful when the Eagles played the Cowboys twice a year.

My dad's parents lived five minutes away, and Friday nights were reserved for Grammy and Pa's house in Nazareth. Grammy and Pa's old stone house, with its steeply sloped Mansard roof, was right next to a deep quarry and a rundown park. It was old, and it was spooky. As kids, we spent countless hours daring each other to venture to the third floor—a dark, cold, and dusty space we were certain was haunted. None of us ever went up there alone, our imaginations running wild with every creak of the floorboards and moving shadow in the dim light.

During the summer months, all the cousins would happily play outside until it was time to watch *The Dukes of Hazzard*. Afterward, we'd be sent back out so the adults could gather in the living room to watch the latest episode of *Dallas*.

Growing up in Tatamy meant being surrounded by family, grounded in a life built on hard work, community, and the simple joys of childhood. My parents and grandparents weren't ones to give grand speeches about life; they simply lived out their values every day. My dad showed it through his dedication to everything he touched, whether it was work, chores around the house, or helping a neighbor rewire their electrical system. My mom, with her warm and welcoming nature, showed it in how she treated everyone around her. Together, they taught us that being true to yourself and treating others with respect were at the core of a good life.

Among my extended family, no one embodied these values more than Pappy. A larger-than-life presence, he was as much a cornerstone of our family as he was of Tatamy itself. Along with my parents, he was a fixture at every football game, wrestling match, baseball game, and soccer game. He was the community leader—President of the Tatamy Fire Company, a member of the Town Council, and active in the Ladies Auxiliary, car shows, carnivals, the Rec Board, and countless community events. He literally had both hands, including his eight and a half fingers, in everything (the other one and a half fingers were lost in a saw accident decades ago).

For his dedication and countless contributions to the Borough of Tatamy and its residents, he was honored with a special day in his name: May 2, 1998—Stuart Albert Day. I don't know about you, but I don't have a day named after me, not even in my own house.

R eligion and the supernatural weren't big topics in our house. We didn't pray at dinner or acknowledge a higher power; we just lived our lives. Technically, we were members of the Lutheran church a hundred yards from our house, but my brother and I went through Bible School and Confirmation more out of tradition than belief. Faith always felt abstract—something intangible and distant— so I didn't spend much time thinking about it.

Even the Bible itself felt like a collection of far-fetched stories to me. Did a giant sea really part in two so people could walk across it? *Come on*. The idea of Marty McFly traveling back in time to the 1950s in a DeLorean seemed more believable than a 600-year-old man building an ark big enough to house all the animals on Earth.

If religion felt abstract, the supernatural seemed downright absurd. To me, it was all nonsense—like the Ouija board that mysteriously showed up at our house one summer. It was just a Hasbro game, for crying out loud—the same company that makes Twister and Hungry Hungry Hippos. The neighborhood kids would drag it out to mess around, asking silly questions like, "Does Amy like me?" and cracking up when the planchette slowly spelled out "NO." It was all fun and games.

Until one night, it wasn't. That was the night my bookshelf came crashing down. I'd stayed up late watching one of those ghost-hunting specials on TV, where paranormal investigators captured eerie noises in abandoned buildings. Those unsettling sounds lingered in my mind as I lay in bed, trying to drift off. Hours later, a deafening crash jolted me awake. My bookshelf had toppled over, scattering books across the room.

The silence that followed was unsettling. No pets, no open windows— nothing that could logically explain the incident. It was probably just a gust of wind or a loose screw in the shelf, I told myself. Shrugging off the unease—though maybe a little spooked—I cleaned up the mess and went back to bed. That was the lens through which I saw the world: if I couldn't hear it, see it, or touch it, it wasn't real.

Even with oddities like that night, my life stayed firmly rooted in the tangible. I got good grades, had a solid group of friends, and spent my time doing classic '80s activities with the neighborhood kids: riding bikes, playing capture the flag in the woods, or heading to the park for pickup games of kickball or wiffle ball. We mostly stayed out of trouble, though there were occasional teenage antics like sneaking beer from the garage refrigerator or making prank calls. By the time I reached high school, my life revolved around sports. Sports became my foundation—a place where discipline, hard work, and clear results mattered above all else.

Wrestling, in particular, gave me a structure that shaped how I tackled challenges, both in high school and later at the Naval Academy. My high school coach, Ray Nunamaker, had coached generations of Nazareth families over his 34-year career, building a tradition of excellence along the way. His coaching career was marked by unbroken success—he never had a losing season, won numerous state titles, and led the 1990–1997 teams to national rankings each year. His most enduring legacy, however, was the philosophy of the 'Circle of Success,' ingrained in every wrestler who passed through the tiny wrestling room next to the gym. Just mention 'The Circle of Success' to anyone who attended Nazareth High School in the last 50 years, and they can likely recite it from memory:

- Believe in Yourself
- Have a Positive Attitude
- Set High Goals
- Have Good Practice Habits
- Perform Well

Coach Nunamaker's Circle Of Success still hangs on the walls decades later

These words resonated so profoundly with me that they not only defined who I was as an athlete, but they also shaped my career approach and later became the baseline of my command philosophy while I was in charge of a squadron.

Central to this philosophy was my belief in mental toughness. It's something I've worked on my entire life, honed through sports, my military experience, and even in family life. The summer before my junior year of high school, I had the chance to attend J. Robinson's Intensive Wrestling Camp at Edinboro University in Northwestern Pennsylvania. Coach Robinson was an Army Ranger, Olympian, and head wrestling coach for the University of Minnesota. His Intensive camps were renowned for pushing wrestlers beyond the limits that exist in your mind, focusing on mental preparation and conditioning while teaching college-level wrestling techniques and practice habits. Coach Robinson and his camp counselors constantly preached discipline, sacrifice, dedication, and hard work, then put us through events that showed us what those words truly meant.

The pre-dawn wake-ups at the camp gave way to Rambo runs, 2 & 1/2 mile-long buddy carries, bleacher runs, and a host of other exercises to greet the sunrise. Three wrestling sessions were scheduled throughout the day, with additional running and calisthenics sprinkled in for good measure.

On the last day of the 14-day camp, we had to run a half marathon. I had never run a half marathon before, and running was never my jam. But I finished with a time under 1:30. When you "graduated" from camp by completing the run, you earned a black t-shirt with the words "I DID IT" printed on the front. Another shirt in the camp store boldly declared "I'm Going to Heaven, 'Cuz I've Been Thru Hell!" across the chest.

I returned from that camp with a completely different perspective on mental toughness.

It was only natural for me to seek opportunities that aligned with my passion for pushing myself to improve through grit and determination. I found that alignment at the United States Naval Academy.

DISCOVERING USNA

My path to the Naval Academy began during my sophomore year of high school. My mom worked for the congressman in our district, and as part of her duties, she organized high school recruiting nights where current cadets and midshipmen would speak to prospective candidates. I didn't grow up around the military, though my dad and grandfather both served in the Army. Little was said about their time in the service, other than the occasional funny story. Consequently, I didn't know much about the military (other than what I'd seen in movies, or on *M.A.S.H.*), and aside from the Army/Navy football game played every December, I couldn't tell you anything about the service academies either.

Though I first started attending these recruiting events to support my mom, the seeds of interest were planted and began to grow. I eventually learned that the United States Naval Academy (USNA) commissions midshipmen as ensigns in the Navy or second lieutenants in the Marine Corps.[1] Midshipmen get to live in Annapolis, MD, and earn a Bachelor of Science degree while being immersed in the military culture and lifestyle that follows graduation.

I think that somewhere inside, there was an underlying call to serve my country, but that wasn't really my main driver at the time. It was the culture that I was seeking, and I was confident that I had the self-belief, attitude, mental toughness, and leadership potential to thrive in that environment.

That same summer of my junior year, after returning from J. Robinson's camp, I sat in the front row of the auditorium at a high school in Bethlehem, PA. It was another recruiting night for the Service Academies, and I was supporting my mom while listening to cadets and midshipmen speak about their experiences. One of the midshipmen from the Naval Academy was a fellow wrestler I'd known for years, and we were able to catch up after the presentation. He was a recruited wrestler at Navy and spoke passionately about his experience there, focusing heavily on the team chemistry in the wrestling room. During our conversation, he offered to connect me with one of the assistant coaches at Navy as soon as he returned to Annapolis.

I was invited to an official recruiting visit later that year, and I was hooked the minute I passed through the gates of "the Yard." The campus was amazing, with views of the water, historic buildings dating back to the 1800s, and a small, close-knit feel that mirrored my high school experiences.

But unlike my small town, there was so much to do and see. Annapolis was just steps from the front gate, and it was unlike any other downtown I had ever seen. Main Street in Tatamy consisted of 6 blocks of small houses built decades ago, while Main Street in Annapolis was full of restaurants, bars, shops, and tons of people out and about.

I also knew I had found a team of people I wanted to be around. During my recruiting visit, I hung out with a great group of Division I wrestlers who were all badasses, and I felt like one of the guys.

There were other recruiting visits during my junior and senior years of high school, but nothing stood out as Navy did.

So, when I opened my Letter of Appointment during my senior year of high school, the joy I felt was overwhelming. If Facebook had existed in the '90s, I would have posted a selfie with a huge grin on my face. All my hard work in high school, the time spent in extracurricular activities, and the months sweating it out in the wrestling room or on the football field…had all paid off because of *my* efforts.

It was a no-brainer: I was headed to the Naval Academy.

CHAPTER 3
I'LL GIVE YOU SOMETHING TO CRY ABOUT

Psalm 56:8 "You keep track of all my sorrows. You have collected all my tears in your bottle. You have recorded each one in your book."

There's a scene in *A League of Their Own* where Coach Jimmy Dugan scolds a player for crying, making it clear that, in his mind, there's no room for tears in baseball. *You know the line.*

Throughout my life, you could substitute just about anything for baseball, and the message would still apply.

In fact, I'm sure many of you can relate to similar sentiments, just expressed differently. Ever heard the phrase, *"Keep crying, and I'll give you something to cry about"*? If you were born in a year that starts with a 19, I'm betting that you have.

Or take *The Great Santini*, where Bull Meechum and his son, Ben, go head-to-head in a heated one-on-one basketball game. When Ben wins, his father doesn't celebrate his victory—instead, he taunts him, calling him a mama's boy, and daring him to squeeze out some tears. *It's a classic scene.*

No matter how you heard it growing up, the message was always the same: tears were for sissies.

When I was six years old, I peed my pants in the middle of my kindergarten class. I have no idea why, it just happened. As the dark spot spread across my brown corduroy pants, I saw classmates elbowing each other with laughter while fingers pointed from every corner of the classroom. I broke down in tears and ran into the hallway, while Ms. D, my kindergarten teacher, stepped out to try to calm me down. Snot ran down my tiny nose, and I stood there sobbing by myself as she walked off to call my mom and ask her to bring new pants.

I don't know whether I was scarred by the act of peeing my pants or by the fact that everyone saw me crying. Probably both.

That same year in kindergarten, I forgot to bring the envelope on picture day, despite our teacher's many reminders not to forget. You remember the envelope…your parents would mark an 'X' in the box next to packages A, B, or C, then put a check inside. Well, when the photographer arrived that day, I reached into my backpack, and the envelope wasn't there. I panicked for reasons I can't explain. Once again, tears started rolling down my face, and my mom had to come to the rescue.

These early experiences of public shame and humiliation stayed with me for a long time, and I remember them vividly as if they happened yesterday. Even after more than 40 years, I can almost see the white, orange, and brown striped shirt I was probably wearing at that time, and still feel the burning sensation in my eyes as I tried my hardest not to cry.

A few years later, around the age of twelve, I attended my first funeral when my dad's father passed away after a long battle with lung cancer. There were a couple of people in the funeral home who stood around like immovable statues, as if they felt no emotion whatsoever. I remember feeling that the tears in my eyes were somehow wrong. I felt conflicted; on one hand, I wanted to act "tough" like they did, but on the other, I couldn't understand how they felt nothing at all. Wasn't this an appropriate time to cry? At that point, I decided I would never let anyone see me cry again, as much as I could help it.

As much as I tried to keep the tears at bay, there were times they came out of nowhere. Sometimes it was the National Anthem. It's pretty embarrassing to be coaching at a youth wrestling tournament, hear the first few notes over the gym loudspeakers, and have to rub your eyes because it hits you right in the soul.

Hearing "Taps" would get me every time, as thoughts of funerals and lost friends rushed back to my mind.

Or when the Budweiser commercial with the Clydesdales and the lost puppy dog came on during the big football game in February, and none of the dudes at the party could make eye contact…

So, yes, I have cried in my life—plenty of times. But the tears always bring feelings of guilt and embarrassment, and that sucks.

Because there's no crying in baseball.

CHAPTER 4
BUILDING ON THE FOUNDATIONS

1 Corinthians 9:24 "*Don't you realize that in a race everyone runs, but only one person gets the prize? So run to win!*"

Friday, July 1, 1994. Early.

As dawn broke, I stood in line with over 1,200 incoming Plebes (freshmen) and their families, waiting to be processed into the Naval Academy Class of 1998. The July heat and humidity in Maryland were already unbearable and sweat pooled under my civilian clothes—the ones I'd soon swap for the "white works" uniform I'd wear for the rest of the summer.

Young men and women from around the world had descended on Annapolis, ready to take on the two-month training program that would test us physically and mentally, preparing us to become midshipmen at the Naval Academy.

In short, it was boot camp.

Calling me nervous is an understatement. The upper-class midshipmen, who would be responsible for our training and well-being that summer, strolled around with confident grins, chatting with the smiling parents standing with us in the long lines. Meanwhile, I felt like my stomach was full of butterflies, knowing those grins would soon turn into shouts and commands.

That morning, I collected armloads of uniforms, socks, shoes, and everything else I'd need for the next seven weeks. I signed what felt like endless forms, made a few new friends, and joked about how much fun this was definitely not going to be.

And, of course, my head was shaved.

With arms stuffed full of gear, we were whisked away in formations of over 30 soon-to-be Plebes and delivered to Bancroft Hall, home to the entire brigade of approximately 4,400 midshipmen and the largest contiguous set of academic dormitories in the U.S., where the training began.

There was so much yelling and chaos—it was complete pandemonium. Push-ups, sit-ups, and sprints filled the rest of the morning. The heat was intense; I was soaked through my uniform within minutes. The first day wasn't even halfway over.

I didn't know any of the other Plebes around me yet, but we were all equally subjected to the wrath of the upperclassmen. As we stood "braced up" against the wall, I heard a girl about five feet away break down in tears.

"There's no crying in Bancroft!" one of the upperclassmen screamed as he got in her face. "Suck it up, Buttercup!"

I'm pretty sure she quit before lunch.

There was a lot to memorize. That first day, as we learned to study our "rates," it was pretty basic: your assigned "alpha code," your room number, and your social security number. You would get asked—well, screamed at—over and over and over again. (Remembering your SSN is harder than you think when you're 18.)

Plebe Summer 1994, Daily Rate Required Reading

At 5:45 that afternoon, we were lined up in formation in the main area in front of Bancroft Hall, which was known then as Tecumseh Court.[1] By 6:00 PM, there was a speech—most of us were too exhausted to pay attention and ended up dozing off—followed by the oath of office. It had been a long, grueling day.

As the days turned into weeks, I quickly found my groove and discovered three things about myself:

1. **My wrestling training had me in prime condition.** I was actually in better shape at the start of Plebe Summer than I was at the end, and was one of the few people to GAIN weight instead of shedding pounds in the summer heat. There were a lot of chicken tenders consumed that summer.

2. **Annapolis is where I was meant to be.** I loved the discipline. The challenge and reward. The people. The camaraderie. I had found my happy place. I had made the right choice. And it was all because *I* worked hard, and *I* deserved it.
3. **Getting yelled at wasn't as bad as I thought it was going to be.** I played Pee Wee football in the '80s, where screwing up meant a coach—usually one who had just stomped out his eighth Marlboro Red of the night—would reach into the huddle, pull you out by your facemask, and bring you within millimeters of his old, sun-beaten leather face while he threatened violence against your tiny body. You had to hold your breath, lest you risk inhaling the puffs of cigarette smoke that spewed from his mouth like an angry dragon.

So, when a 20-year-old who only shaves once a week starts yelling about putting your socks away correctly, it's pretty easy to block it out. In fact, it's hard not to laugh.

I had no idea why some of these plebes were struggling. Some of these kids here just needed to suck it up.

Induction Day Ceremony - July 1, 1994

CHAPTER 5
SUCK IT UP, BUTTERCUP

1 Corinthians 15:10 *"But whatever I am now, it is all because God poured out his special favor on me—and not without results. For I have worked harder than any of the other apostles; yet it was not I but God who was working through me by his grace."*

That first day at the Naval Academy was not the first time I heard "Suck it up, Buttercup." I don't remember when I first heard it, but it was a mantra drilled into my head early in life.

Anecdotally, the origin of the phrase dates back to World War II as guidance for pilots in the event they threw up mid-flight while wearing oxygen masks. Even if that's not the real origin—and Reddit got it wrong again—I'm sticking with it anyway. Everyone says it, usually in jest, but it captures the mindset of pushing through adversity. It's a reminder that someone needs to be mentally tough, especially if they are complaining about something.

I heard it constantly at the Naval Academy. These four words were screamed in my face countless times throughout my first year, especially during Plebe Summer.

The phrase was just as rampant in my first squadron, mostly from my good friend Steve, who jokingly poked fun at anyone who complained about anything.

While writing this chapter, I searched my text messages for "Suck it up, Buttercup," just for fun. I found two separate group threads where that phrase was used, all in jest, of course.

Check your text messages…I bet you'll find the same thing

So what does it really mean? It underscores the idea of pushing through emotional barriers to focus on the task at hand. It says, "Hey man, whatever might seem 'difficult' to you right now isn't. Just forget about it, and let's go do this."

Don't get me wrong. I'm not saying it's a bad thing. In our everyday lives, we NEED to just suck it up and move on. We can't be a society of people who roll over and quit whenever times get a little tough. I don't want to see my favorite Philadelphia athletes sitting out the season because of a little booboo.[1]

Imagine a press conference where your team's starting QB comes on and says, "Hey everybody, my pinky toe is a bit sore, so I'm going to sit this playoff game out." Likewise, I don't want my children to learn that they can just skip practice if their pinky toe hurts, even just a little.

But where exactly is that line between sucking it up and asking for help, or even just taking a breather? We tend to think about the physical aspect of pain and the mind's ability to compartmentalize to push through it. But how do you evaluate your pain and decide what to do? Most people probably ask themselves: Will continuing cause long-term or irreversible damage, or is it just a short-term, nagging pain? And how critical is the task—am I on a casual Saturday morning jog where my knee hurts and running will only make it worse, or is this the final playoff game of the year, where I won't get another shot?

Pushing past pain and fatigue was just something we did. When I was 14, I was riding bikes with my best friend, Jake. We thought we were cool and doing some high-speed runs at a quarter pipe. After a jump went wrong, I left a few feet of skin on the blacktop as blood ran down my arms and legs. It really, really hurt. I can still hear the echoing of the neighborhood kids, yelling "Suck it up! Suck it up!" I did what most kids would do: got back on, straightened the handlebars, and kept riding.

Think back to Coach Ray Nunamaker's Circle of Success... I believed in myself. I had a positive attitude. Think about Coach J. Robinson showing me how to push myself beyond limits that existed in my mind. As a teenager, I wore the "I'm Going To Heaven, 'Cus I've Been Thru Hell" t-shirt all the time. It was part of what made me who I am.

But what about pushing through mental pain? What about sucking it up through emotional trauma, or even those tiny, little everyday stressors that have an impact on your emotional health? When is it time to shove the thoughts down and move on, and when is it time to address the pain and reach out for help?

Nobody ever teaches us how to do that. And if somebody did, I probably wasn't listening.

CHAPTER 6
LIFE AS A MIDSHIPMAN

Revelation 3:8 *"I know all the things you do, and I have opened a door for you that no one can close."*

It's hard to compare the Naval Academy to a "normal" college because it's just not the same. Sure, every college has its challenges, and you can make lifelong friends anywhere. But at the Academy, those bonds form differently. The stakes are higher, the pressure never lets up, and you're not just studying for exams—you're training for something real. When there is an expectation that one day you could be asked to sacrifice your own life for others, that kind of trust runs deeper. It's not just friendship; it's knowing that you have to rely on each other in ways no textbook could ever prepare you for.

There were plenty of ways to escape the challenges of the classroom and the halls. On Sundays, we could attend church services, but that wasn't for me. Why waste your time in church when you could be doing anything else, like sleeping?

But, I learned that joining the church choir got you out of getting yelled at. So, I gave singing a shot. A sign-up sheet was posted in the main hallway outside our dorm rooms, and I put my name down— fully aware that I couldn't sing. Not even a little.

Growing up, there weren't any reality TV singing shows, and I'd never tried out for anything in my life. So when I showed up to the audition, expecting they would just group a few of us together to sing "Jingle Bells" or something, I was pretty shocked when the director asked, "What will you be singing for us?"

I panicked. I couldn't think of a single song whose lyrics I could remember—except maybe 2 Live Crew,[1] which definitely wouldn't have been appropriate in the Chapel. For some reason, I blurted out "The Navy Hymn," a song I'd heard countless times that summer. The first verse goes:

> Eternal Father, strong to save,
> Whose arm hath bound the restless wave,
> Who bidd'st the mighty ocean deep
> Its own appointed limits keep,
> O hear us when we cry to thee
> For those in peril on the sea!

I don't know why, but I couldn't get through it. Not entirely because of my singing (though that didn't help), but because I kept choking up. Every time I started singing, my eyes welled with tears. I fought them off as best I could, but my voice cracked, and I probably sounded like an idiot.

Somehow, I was accepted into the choir, though I'm still not sure why —I wouldn't have said yes, but maybe they were desperate. So, I showed up to every summer practice, escaping the madness and chaos of the halls. And every Sunday, I stood with the other Plebes during Mass, belting out that same song, trying not to cry in front of the other midshipmen.

Once the school year started, I had enough of that nonsense—because I was there to wrestle.

There was something about that environment that pushed me to my limits and made me strive for improvement.

The lessons I learned on the wrestling mat at age five followed me through college and still stick with me today. Wrestling tests your mental toughness every time you lace up your shoes and step onto the mat. There's no teammate to blame for missing a block, no coach who called the wrong play, and there are no backups coming in to give you a breather. It's just you and your opponent, and the better man wins. The one who works harder. The one who puts in the time. The one with the winning mindset. The one who sucks it up when things get tough and pushes beyond his own mental limits.

To be clear, I was a very average Division I wrestler. Though I lettered for three years and got plenty of matches under my belt, I ended up missing most of my junior year due to a back injury. That injury was one of the first times I felt "gaslit," though I didn't know the term at the time. Years later, my wife would use it to describe her experiences with doctors—going in with a legitimate issue, only to be told she was "normal," leaving her to question whether her symptoms were real.

My injury wasn't one of those dramatic moments where I screamed and fell over in pain during practice. I vaguely remember "tweaking" something during a spring workout in my sophomore year. No big deal—I shook it off and kept going. It wasn't a ton of pain, certainly not enough to see a trainer.

The next day, my lower back was killing me. It took a few minutes before I could stand up straight—kinda like when you spend the day working on flowerbeds in the backyard, and the next morning, you pay for it because you haven't used those muscles in a while. But I had been using those muscles every day, so that wasn't the issue.

I sucked it up, carefully went about my day, and returned to the wrestling room for practice after my last class. The stiffness had eased a bit by the afternoon, and I felt better.

The next morning, though, it was the same story. Only this time, it took me even longer to stand up straight.

As the days went by, it took even longer to stand up straight throughout the day. Eventually, I decided to see the trainer, who referred me to the team orthopedic doctor. By then, the pain was constant, and I couldn't run or make any sudden movements—things that are essential in wrestling.

The diagnosis was some kind of muscle strain, and the treatment plan included strengthening exercises and Flexeril to manage the muscle spasms. But the pain never fully went away unless I was on the pills, and as it continued through the summer and into the fall, I ended up missing most of my junior year. It was one of the first times in my life that I couldn't push through the pain, no matter how hard I tried. I was like the old man constantly complaining about his back, but I was 21 years old. It made me feel weak.

Throughout the fall, I either sat along the wall during practice or hopped on a bike, watching my teammates work their butts off. I was embarrassed when people asked, "What's wrong with you?" only to reply, "...I don't know, my back hurts...."

The look on their faces was always the same: "Such a wuss."

In late December of my junior year, over Christmas break, I was back in PA, spending time with family. When I wrestled at Nazareth High School, an alumnus and former heavyweight regularly stopped by the room to work out with our bigger guys, and he also happened to be a chiropractor. He made it clear to everybody in the room that we were welcome to stop by his office anytime—no appointment needed. Desperate for a fix to my back pain, I took him up on that. And after just 30 seconds on his table, he said, "Oh, feels like your hip is rotated out of place. Here, let's do this:"

POP! That was the sound of immediate relief. Finally, someone acknowledged my pain and helped me fix it. However, that year was already written off for me in the room, as I was far behind in my conditioning and still had a lot of physical therapy to get my lower back feeling good again.

My senior year arrived and this time I was a regular starter, traveling with the team and competing all around the East Coast while proudly wearing the Navy singlet. I was having a so-so year competing, but I was having a lot of fun with the team and looking forward to the post-season tournaments. Toward the end of the regular season, I felt and heard a muffled pop in my right shoulder during a match in the room. "Damn, that hurt." I got up and shook it off, knowing that nothing was dislocated or torn, and continued with the rest of practice.

The next day, I couldn't lift my arm past 90 degrees, so I went to see our trainer. After diagnosing me with a common muscle strain, I was given the standard post-injury protocol: rest, ice, stretching, and strengthening. No matter what I tried, I couldn't make my shoulder recover quickly enough to compete in the national qualifier at the end of the season.

I share this not to assign blame to doctors, trainers, or any medical professionals. Instead, I want to illustrate how I continued to push my discomfort aside to compete, trying my best to suck it up and not cry about it, yet there were times I couldn't succeed. This began to chip away at my self-confidence, bringing self-doubt into play. In a sense, I was gaslighting my own body and mind, convincing myself that there was nothing wrong while feeling shame for even asking the questions in the first place.

But despite all that, I kept pushing forward. Wrestling was such a significant part of my Naval Academy experience, and the discipline I learned there made me think I wanted to become a Navy SEAL. I mean, who doesn't? They're a bunch of badasses, and I thought I was one too.

We had a Navy SEAL officer on staff who ran our conditioning program. It was challenging, and we all had the same love/hate relationship with the work that we were doing. Training with our Navy conditioning coach brought back memories from J. Robinson's camp, where I pushed myself harder and harder until I experienced breakthroughs. All of this, combined with the camaraderie and the overall mission of the Navy SEALs, made me eager to try to join their ranks.

So I set my sights on becoming a member of the Navy's elite special forces unit…

And then, I jumped into the pool.

It didn't make sense. I practically lived at my grandparents' pool. I could hold my breath underwater and do backflips off the diving board, so I thought I was a decent swimmer—until a few experiences made me rethink that. Playing a pickup game of water polo (who plays a sport where you try to drown people?) was one. Then came swim classes in PE, which made me realize I hated swimming. That feeling was confirmed when the wrestling team started water conditioning. It felt pointless—I never finished a match thinking, *"Man, if only I had swum harder, I could have scored more points."*

If I didn't enjoy being in the water, perhaps pursuing a SEAL career wasn't an option for me.

I considered becoming a Marine. I admired their values of honor, courage, and commitment. Their uniforms always looked crisp. Every Marine I'd met was motivated, tough as nails, and passionate about their profession.

Then I attended summer training at Quantico. While I enjoyed the physical aspects and loved being outside in nature, it just didn't align with my personality or what I was seeking. There was too much yelling and everything felt too high-strung. I had just completed my plebe year, enduring the constant screaming and yelling with upper-classman in my face, and it was starting to wear on me. In fact, I was caught snickering a couple of times when the drill sergeants were on a roll, which only made things worse for me. But some of the things they said were genuinely funny!

One rainy afternoon, while we were out in the field practicing camou-flage and concealment, we were instructed to find natural materials to help disguise our profiles. My buddy Lance found two branches that looked exactly like deer antlers. He stuck them in his helmet, painted his face brown, used berries to stain his nose, and started prancing around the woods of Quantico, singing *"Rudolph the Red-Nosed Reindeer."*

I couldn't stop laughing, which definitely caught the attention of the drill sergeants. They didn't find it nearly as funny, and let's just say, there were a lot of push-ups that afternoon.

Once again, it was another door that wasn't meant for me.

Navy wrestling photo and Marine summer training

With that door closed, I still needed to figure out my career path. If I claimed that *Top Gun* was a major influence on my decision, I'd be stretching the truth. I was around 11 when the movie came out, and I watched it a few times throughout my childhood. Flying seemed pretty cool—far better than ships or submarines—so I set my sights on aviation.

When I was 16, during a routine physical exam in high school, the doctor informed me that I needed glasses.

"For what?" I asked. "I can see perfectly well."

"Well, your left eye is fine, but your right eye is about 20/40. I can get you a pair of glasses with one prescription lens and the other just clear."

"That sounds stupid," I thought. *"Why would I wear glasses just to see the same way I do without them?"*

So, I took my new half-glasses home and tossed them into a drawer, not thinking much about them until my aviation physical. During that examination, the Navy doctor informed me that I was "Not Physically Qualified" to be a pilot.

What? Is it the same situation all over again? I can see perfectly well with both eyes open! WHEN WILL I EVER HAVE TO CLOSE MY LEFT EYE AND JUST FLY WITH MY RIGHT ONE OPEN? This is ridiculous.

Another door had closed.

The next logical option was Naval Flight Officer (NFO). To qualify for an NFO position, your vision had to be correctable to 20/20 or better in each eye. *Check*! NFOs specialize in managing airborne weapons, sensor systems, and mission functions, depending on the aircraft they fly. There are various titles and roles, like Electronic Warfare Officer (EWO), Weapon Systems Officer (WSO), navigator, and battle manager. In *Top Gun*, Goose was an NFO (referred to as a Radar Intercept Officer in the F-14), and in *Top Gun: Maverick*, Bob and Fanboy were both WSOs.

This still sounded pretty cool. Sure, I wouldn't be at the controls, but I'd still be in the cockpit, riding backseat in a high-speed fighter jet— just like Goose.

One night in February 1998, when it was my turn for Service Selection, I headed down to Smoke Hall just a floor below the Rotunda in Bancroft Hall. Midshipmen were called down by their Order of Merit, an overall class ranking based on academic, military, and athletic performance. And as long as you passed all the pre-qualifications for the different career paths, you could choose what you wanted right there on the spot. I was right in the middle of the pack, and there were only so many NFO slots available each year. After hitting all the marks, passing the medical exams, and getting the green light to join the program, I approached the big board hoping to see slots still open. If not, I'd have to choose something else.

Thankfully, there were spots still up for grabs. And while this wasn't my first, second, or even third choice, the door I was meant to walk through was labeled "Naval Flight Officer," with a class start date of November 2, 1998. Next stop: Pensacola, FL, the "Cradle of Naval Aviation" and the launching point for the flight training of every Naval Aviator, Flight Officer, and enlisted aircrewman. [2]

CHAPTER 7
TAKING FLIGHT

Philippians 1:6 "*And I am certain that God, who began the good work within you, will continue his work until it is finally finished on the day when Christ Jesus returns.*"

Sunday, November 1, 1998. 4:30 PM

I graduated from the Naval Academy in May of 1998, and after getting "stashed" on the yard for about 5 months, I was ready to check in for ground school and kickstart my aviation career.

Four of us made the sixteen-hour drive from Annapolis, MD, to the beautiful beaches of Perdido Key, Florida. In reality, we completed the drive in less than fourteen hours, driving straight through the night and stopping only for gas and food. There's no chance I could do that now in my adult life.

Perdido Key is a narrow strip of land in the Florida Panhandle, situated between Pensacola and Orange Beach, Alabama, making it a perfect spot for a couple of young twenty-something men fresh out of the Naval Academy to start "adulting." Pensacola is just a few miles away and has a proud military heritage that dates back to the early 1900s. Naval Air Station Pensacola is home to approximately 16,000 military members and houses the Naval Education and Training

Command, multiple training squadrons, and, of course, the world-famous Blue Angels.[1]

The only hiccup we encountered was finding a place to live after discovering that Hurricane Georges had devastated the townhouse where we had put down a deposit months earlier. That hurricane ended up saving both my liver and my wallet, as the townhouse was located directly across the street from the legendary Flora-Bama beach bar and just a stone's throw away from a nearby Waffle House. Between the booze and the late-night smothered-and-covered break-fasts, I don't think I would have survived flight school. Call it luck, fate, or just a happy accident, but the universe was looking out for me.

Fortunately, the realtor found a replacement condo for us. Although we had to wait a few weeks for the previous tenants to move out, we managed to make do with a fully furnished beach rental, where the patio doors opened to the beautiful shores of the Gulf of Mexico.

The initial training, called Aviation Pre-flight Indoctrination (API), lasted a few months and introduced aviation principles, weather, flight rules, and basic aircraft systems for all pilots and NFOs. After completing API, I spent the next year at VT-4, one of the two primary aircraft training squadrons at the time. I learned to fly the T-34 Mentor —a prop-driven, single-engine military trainer—before transitioning to the T-1A Jayhawk—a twin-engine jet—where I honed my navigation skills in low-level environments during Intermediate training.[2]

Me & Pappy on the flight line in Pensacola

Me & my mom in Pensacola

In the Navy, I used to joke that I never got my first choice in anything, yet the option handed to me always worked out in my favor. "Big Navy" clearly knew better, so I learned to trust their judgment over mine. It's like going on a hike and seeing two paths, both leading to different peaks with views of the same valley. You can't go wrong with either, but for some reason, you want to take the path on the left because it seems more fun. Just before you take your first step, the park ranger steps out from behind a tree and says, "Hey man, the path on the left is closed, you can only take the one on the right. It'll be fine."

With Intermediate training complete, it was time to make a choice that would define my future in the aviation community. I had two paths ahead of me:

- Select jets, and on Monday morning check in to VT-86, the jet training squadron next door, where I would learn the T-2C Buckeye on my way to an F-14 Tomcat or EA-6B Prowler squadron.

- Or, move to Norfolk and become an E-2C Hawkeye Naval Flight Officer.

You're probably asking, "What's an E-2C Hawkeye?"

Great question, because I had the same one. I had never heard of the Hawkeye, never seen it in person, and it wasn't the featured airplane in any Hollywood film. I'd heard something about a couple of propellers and that it was carrier-based, but that's about it. The internet wasn't really a thing yet, so my information came from the photos that lined the squadron hallways, and whatever I could get from the flight instructors. I guess I could've gone to the library to check out a book, too.

The E-2C Hawkeye

Obviously, I wanted jets, and the F-14 Tomcat was the clear choice. *Top Gun* was a few years in the rearview mirror, but the F-14 was still the coolest plane available for Naval Flight Officers—or so I thought at the time.[3]

As graduation day approached, it came down to the wire with only four students moving on that Friday from Intermediate to Advanced training. Word on the street was that there was one spot for the E-2C Hawkeye, which had to be filled, while the rest were for jet spots. As a general rule, the student with the highest flight school grades received their first choice.

Spoiler alert: that student wasn't me.

Of the four students who were scheduled to show up in a fancy uniform on Friday, this is how it went:

The first student, the guy with the big brain, chose jets as his first choice.

The second student "failed" his evaluation check-ride the day before, so he was rolled into the next class that would graduate in a few weeks. Oddly enough, there were no E-2C Hawkeye spots available for that class. *Strange.* I mean, I'm sure he didn't fail on purpose, right? (We're actually good friends, but he still won't admit it publicly!)

The third student was from the South African Air Force, sent to the U.S. as part of an ongoing exchange program. I assumed he would NOT show up that morning, rip off his South African Air Force patches, and declare his allegiance to the United States by demanding to be a U.S. Navy E-2C Naval Flight Officer…

That left one spot to be filled in Norfolk—and one student left to fill it: me.

I still held on to a glimmer of hope—maybe they'd open up another jet slot, or perhaps the Navy would unexpectedly decide to retire the E-2 by the end of the week. But when the squadron Commanding Officer walked into the ready room with folders in hand, it became clear where we all stood. Two were thin, while the third was noticeably thicker, clearly filled with "Welcome to Norfolk" materials for the lucky candidate. Everyone else received a certificate of graduation from VT-4, a handshake, and a patch from VT-86.

So, I was finished with my journey in Pensacola, and it was time to head to Norfolk, Virginia, to start my training in the E-2C Hawkeye. As a bonus, I would meet my future wife, Eleanor, in a food court.

Pappy, my dad, and my mom at my winging ceremony

CHAPTER 8
A CHANCE ENCOUNTER

Genesis 2:18 *"Then the Lord God said, 'It is not good for the man to be alone. I will make a helper who is just right for him.'"*

Thursday, March 16, 2000. 12:30 PM

M ike and I sat in the food court at Naval Station Norfolk, wolfing down Taco Bell between classes and a simulator session scheduled for later that day.

I first met Mike back in Pensacola, and now we were both part of the same training class at VAW-120, the E-2 Fleet Replacement Squadron.

We'd been in Norfolk for about six months, shifting from a classroom-focused syllabus to more hands-on training. It was challenging but enjoyable.

"Hey, I know that girl," Mike said, peering over my shoulder into the crowded food court.

"Who?" I asked. He gestured vaguely toward a group of people in uniform, but I had no idea who he meant. I stayed focused on my beef taco, not really interested.

"Hey, Eleanor!" Mike shouted, and I turned to see who had grabbed his attention. A girl in uniform approached our table, looking a bit awkward as Mike fired off questions. "What are you doing here? I haven't seen you in ages! Where are you living? A bunch of us are going out tomorrow night—why don't you join us?"

She answered his questions, though somewhat reluctantly, and throughout the conversation I learned that she had recently moved to the area to join her first ship in the Navy, and was clearly working way harder than we were. She agreed to call Mike later before saying goodbye and heading back to work.

"Who was that?" I asked once she was out of sight.

"Oh, she was in my ROTC unit at Carnegie Mellon, but she was a year behind me," Mike explained. [1]

"And... what? You think she's going to come 'hang out' with us idiots?" I asked. "I wouldn't."

"Who knows." Mike shrugged. We finished lunch and headed back to the simulator building.

As it turned out, she did decide to join us, which worked out well for me. And, as luck would have it, that night it was my turn to be the designated driver.

Friday night, nine of us gathered at Mike's apartment to pregame. There were two girls there—one was a classmate from VAW-120, and the other was Eleanor. Six of us crammed into Mike's Jeep Cherokee, with me behind the wheel, and headed downtown to Norfolk while the rest took a taxi to meet us there.

Nothing particularly wild happened that night. It was just a bunch of aviation students blowing off steam at a bar called Have A Nice Day Cafe in downtown Norfolk. While some in the group indulged a bit more than others, I stayed calm, cool, and collected, playing the role of the sober driver. Eleanor and I spent the night talking, dancing, and getting to know each other, and I silently thanked the universe for making me the designated driver, sparing me from getting as Thunderdome drunk as my friends. If I hadn't drawn the lucky DD straw, I probably would've been right there with them.

Last call came way too soon, and as we hit the exits, one of the guys in the group begged us to stop at a hot dog stand outside the bar for some late-night snacks. That would turn out to be a poor decision for all of us.

About 20 minutes later I was driving us home on I-264, the highway empty at this hour, with Eleanor in the passenger seat beside me. Three guys were in the back, doing what drunk guys do—telling stories, singing, and laughing at us up front. About halfway home, my friend Chris, who was sitting directly behind me, groaned, "Man... I'm not feeling so good."

"Suck it up, man, we're almost home," I yelled back.

"Dude, roll down the window," Mike shouted. "Don't puke in my Jeep!"

Chris seemed to hear Mike's advice. But his execution was lagging, and unfortunately for all of us, he didn't actually roll the window down at all.

"Nope. Not gonna maaaak..." was all we heard before the unmistakable sound of regret hit the glass, followed by the stench of regurgitated potato chips.

There was no point in pulling over now. I kept driving as the remnants of his late-night snack streaked down the window and soaked into the gray carpet. The rest of the ride was eerily quiet—both up front and in the back.

When we finally made it back to Mike's apartment, it wasn't surprising that Eleanor called it a night.

I was sure that would be the last time I'd see her.

CHAPTER 9
THINGS CHANGE

Proverbs 16:1 *"We can make our own plans, but the Lord gives the right answer."*

2001-2003

Fortunately for me, that wasn't the last time I saw Eleanor. A few days later, I called her to say I had a great time and, of course, to apologize for my crazy friends, assuring her that what she saw wasn't really who we were.

I was kind of stretching the truth. I mean, come on, we were flight school students in our early 20s, getting paid to study, fly, and hang out with our best friends. Life was awesome. Every weekend ended with a pretty good story to share in the ready room on Monday. But she didn't need to hear that; she just needed to hear how responsible I was and that I was a pretty good guy.

Over the next couple of months, Eleanor and I continued to hang out more and more. But then it came time for her to deploy on the ship she was assigned to. It was going to be a six-month deployment, and as she was leaving, I had every intention of seeing this relationship continue to blossom. As she left, I promised to wait for her and to be there when she got back.

But I was stupid, and I didn't keep those promises. About a month after she left, I met someone else, and that girl became my new first choice. In the ultimate cowardly move, I sent Eleanor an email to end the relationship.

When Eleanor returned from her deployment, I wasn't on the pier waiting for her like I said I would be. But I'd see her around town from time to time—like one night at my favorite bar, The Hot Tuna. She was pissed, and so were her friends. I don't blame them. I might have even had a drink thrown at me that night, and it was well deserved. But at that point in my life, I thought I had made the right choice.

I carried on with life, focusing much of my time on studying and learning the airplane. As my training at VAW-120 neared its end, it was time to figure out where I would begin my first operational tour and which fleet squadron I would be assigned to.

In Naval Aviation, there's a traditional path that takes you from flight school student to Commanding Officer, a journey that spans roughly 17 years. Your first squadron is where you truly cut your teeth, flying real-world missions and mastering the ins and outs of your aircraft. This first tour is all about gaining experience, sharpening your skills, and proving yourself as a fleet operator.

In addition to flying, you're assigned a "ground job," which gives you a taste of leadership as you rotate through divisions like Maintenance, Operations, Safety, Training, or Admin. Responsibilities increase as you gain more experience.

It's a period of intense learning and growth, where you're expected to quickly become an expert in your aircraft and a trusted member of the squadron.

In my flight school class of 10 students, we had 5 spots for Norfolk, 1 for Japan, and 4 for the West Coast in Point Mugu, California (where even is that?). As an East Coast guy, the idea of heading to some place in California I'd never heard of didn't appeal to me at all, and I definitely didn't want to leave the country. So, I had my fingers crossed for one of the Norfolk spots.

Me, 1999: *Hey Navy, I'd really like to stay in Norfolk. I just met this girl, and I'm enjoying it here, so if we could just avoid any moves, that'd be awesome. Thanks.*

Navy: *Nope, pack your bags—you're headed to Naval Air Station Point Mugu, California.*[1]

And so, off to the West Coast I went. The girl I'd tried to stay in Norfolk for dumped me just a few weeks after I settled in California. I took it hard—probably as hard as Eleanor had when I broke my promises to her. It was February 2001, just seven months before 9/11 would change the world forever.

September 10th was business as usual. But the next day, Tuesday, everything changed. At the time, my good friend Pat and I shared a condo in Newbury Park, about 20 minutes from the base. Just before 6 AM West Coast time, we were sound asleep when the phone rang. It was Pat's girlfriend (now wife) on the phone, calling to alert us that something had happened in New York City. We turned the news on and started getting ready to head in for the day. Then the second plane struck the South Tower, and the phone rang again. This time, it was our squadron duty office, telling us to get to base—immediately. We threw on our flight suits, jumped into my car, and raced to the base without a second thought. Speeding wasn't a concern that day—I figured we had a good excuse.

When we reached the base gate, the line of cars waiting to get in stretched about half a mile. *"Screw it,"* I thought, *"we're going to the front."* I swerved around the long line of civilians heading to work, flashers on, windows down, praying nobody would start shooting at us. We got close to the front when a security guard stopped us, his weapon aimed roughly in our direction.

"Our squadron called!" I shouted, holding up my ID. "We need to get planes in the air—now!" He checked my ID, saw I wasn't a threat, and waved us through.

As soon as enough pilots and NFOs showed up to fill out a crew, we started jumping into airplanes. While we were taking off, we learned that further attacks were likely on the West Coast, although the specific targets were unknown. My crew was ordered to patrol the skies between Los Angeles and San Francisco and direct sections of fighters to assist with visual identification if needed. At that point, the airspace around the U.S. had been shut down, and all civilian aircraft had been ordered to land at the nearest airport. In the most chilling radio call I've ever heard, we received authorization to shoot down any aircraft believed to be hijacked or unresponsive to radio calls.[2]

Holy crap. We had trained to identify and target hostile aircraft in a wartime scenario, but this wasn't in the training manual. There were some very close calls that day—extremely close calls.

We were airborne for over ten hours on September 11th, only stopping to refuel about five hours into the flight. That night, I slept under my desk in the hangar, my head resting on a pile of t-shirts, waiting to see where we would be needed next.

Seven days later, on September 18, our Air Wing accelerated the training cycle to get ready for a combat deployment that we all knew was coming but wasn't officially announced. We spent a month in Fallon, Nevada before making final preparations to join the USS John C. Stennis Strike Group at sea. And by November 1st, we were underway and headed west.

I was new to the squadron and still finding my way in the Navy, but this was exactly what I had prepared for my entire life. It was time to compartmentalize, focus, and answer the nation's call. It may sound cliché, but I felt immense pride in what I was doing. During those early days of Operation Enduring Freedom, with round-the-clock sorties over the skies of Afghanistan, the days and nights were long, but I was proud to be part of it all.

Six months later, we returned to Point Mugu, California, knowing we would soon turn around and do it all over again. However, we had some downtime before resuming training in October. During that break, an opportunity arose to attend a wedding back in Norfolk. So, five of us loaded up an E-2 and headed east for some "training." While I was there, I took the chance to reconnect with Eleanor. For some reason, she decided to give me another chance, and we went out to dinner when I got into town. That was the start of a renewed relationship—this time with the added difficulty of living on opposite coasts.

Whenever we had free weekends, which were few and far between at that point in our lives, we made it a priority to see each other as much as possible. When it came time for me to move on from my first squadron, I was once again faced with a choice: A) focus on my career and take one of the jobs along the path the Navy wanted, or B) be reunited with my girlfriend.

The Navy wanted A, but I wanted B. The solution would lie somewhere in between.

We all know stories about people who meet and instantly realize they are soulmates, as if their meeting was destined. Maybe you have one of those stories. I didn't have that realization right away—my journey was marked by mistakes and detours.

I had yet to understand that someone else was calling the shots for me and determining my path. And though it took moving to California to truly see it, everything was leading me back to Eleanor, the person I was always meant to be with.

CHAPTER 10
BOXES IN THE CLOSET

Exodus 18:17-18 *"This is not good!" Moses' father-in-law exclaimed. "You're going to wear yourself out—and the people, too. This job is too heavy a burden for you to handle all by yourself."*

Now that I was establishing myself in my military career, I had gotten good at multitasking. I had also become very good at compartmentalizing. But what's the difference between the two?

People multitask all the time. Think about the simple task of driving a car: you're keeping your eyes on the road, observing other drivers, asking Siri to send a text, adjusting the temperature—all while chatting with your spouse on the way to Costco on a Saturday morning.

Pilots multitask too. Picture the cockpit of an airplane: pilots are monitoring aircraft systems and instruments, communicating with air traffic control, and making real-time adjustments to fly from point A to point B.

In the E-2C Hawkeye, multitasking is taken to another level. With its advanced communication suite, NFOs learn to listen to two or three radios simultaneously, talk on the fourth and fifth radios, direct fighter aircraft toward a target, coordinate with ships and aerial refueling assets, and communicate with crew members over the internal comms —all at once.

But compartmentalizing is different. While multitasking is about juggling tasks, compartmentalizing is about shutting out mental distractions, allowing you to focus and elevate both mind and body to a heightened level of concentration.

Imagine boarding a plane in Dallas after a long day of weather delays and gate changes. You finally settle into seat 33B, sandwiched between the big dude on your left, and Mr. Farts-a-lot on your right, but still relieved to finally be heading home. Then, the pilot comes on the PA and says: "Welcome aboard, everyone. This is your Captain speaking. Just wanted to let you know I'm having a really bad day. A few minutes ago, my wife texted me—and…apparently, she's leaving me, taking the three kids with her, and she told me not to look for her. Oh, and she cleared out our bank accounts. And, on the way out the door, she kicked my dog so hard that she broke all 26 of his ribs. So, there's that vet bill too. But don't worry, I'll compartmentalize, suck it up, and focus on flying us safely to Chicago. Our flight time today is two hours and thirteen minutes, and did you know that you can earn 75,000 miles today if you…"

Wait. What?

Within 45 seconds, I'd expect the entire plane to empty—passengers sliding down the emergency chutes if they had to.

But now, replace that 737 with a military aircraft. And swap out Chicago for a foreign land, where the lives of soldiers on the ground depend on you to get that jet airborne. When the mission is saving lives and winning in combat, there is no room for outside distractions.

This casts compartmentalizing into a whole new light. It's about taking the distractions, your emotions, and all of life's stressors, placing them in a box, shelving that box in the closet of your mind, and closing the door—so you can focus entirely on the job in front of you.

Growing up, I embraced the "suck it up" mentality. Whether it was on the football field, in the wrestling room, in the classroom, or later in the military, I absorbed the message that real men don't show weakness. If something was bothering me, I sucked it up and moved on. After all, there's no crying in baseball, and there's certainly no crying in the military.

In doing so, I mastered the skill of compartmentalizing. That's how I dealt with sickness, pain, and even death. However, I never truly learned what to do next. I was excellent at shoving boxes into the closet, but I didn't know how to return and examine the contents later.

I suspect most of us aren't taught or shown how to deal with our emotional boxes, so we just keep piling them up until there's no more room. When that happens, something has to give.

And that is one of the reasons why, 41 years after I peed my pants in kindergarten, I lost my cool on an employee for no reason whatsoever. I know I haven't told you that story yet, but it's coming.

CHAPTER 11
DC TOUR & MORE

Mark 10:8-9 "*…and the two will become one flesh. So they are no longer two, but one flesh. Therefore what God has joined together, let no one separate.*" *(NIV)*

Saturday, October 9, 2004. 4:30 PM

It was a beautiful October day just outside Baltimore, Maryland. As I stood at the altar, waiting for my soon-to-be wife to walk down the aisle, I beamed with pride, trying to keep my nerves in check. More than 100 of our closest family and friends had gathered for the weekend, and the setting at Celebrations at the Bay was simply picturesque.

The sweeping views of the Chesapeake Bay provided a stunning backdrop for our wedding. Eleanor and I had spent months exploring venues before finally settling on this one. The wedding was outdoors, and I stood beneath a flower arch that a few of my aunts had spent hours crafting.

Our wedding day

We decided against a traditional church ceremony—neither of us was particularly drawn to the formality, and it had been years since either of us had set foot in a church. Still, we weren't exactly eager to admit that to the pastor we asked to officiate our wedding. Somehow, we convinced a Naval Academy pastor to perform an off-site wedding, framing it as a desire to celebrate God's creation with an outdoor ceremony, rather than opting for the traditional Academy Chapel setting. Outside the confines of the church, we also enjoyed the freedom to pass out cocktails before the ceremony began.

To show our appreciation, we made sure to take good care of him for his efforts—or so I thought at the time. Looking back, I'm embarrassed by how small the "donation" we left for him actually was. I think I've left better tips at Olive Garden.

But the road to that altar, where I stood nervously waiting for Eleanor, wasn't exactly straightforward. Almost a year earlier, I had left Point Mugu for Maryland. If you'd told that younger version of me—especially the one sitting in a Taco Bell food court with my buddy Mike—that I'd someday be in the D.C. area, waiting for this incredible woman to walk out of a bridal suite in her gorgeous wedding gown, I wouldn't have believed it.

After spending about three years in your first operational squadron, it's time to move on to stay on 'the path' toward your next career milestone: becoming a squadron Department Head. The aviation community places particular value on certain key roles, such as attending advanced training schools or taking on instructor positions. These include places like the Naval Aviation Warfighting Development Center (NAWDC) in Fallon, NV—home of TOPGUN—or returning to the training command for your specific aircraft.

Of all the roles the aviation community held in high regard, I wasn't interested in a single one of them.

The last two years had been a whirlwind, and I was completely in love. So much so that I didn't care about my career at all—I just wanted my first-choice assignment, and I wanted it to be with her.

As I wrapped up my time at Point Mugu, trying to figure out my next move, I found myself wrestling with second-choice struggles while navigating conversations with the Navy.

Me, 2003: *So, Navy, it's been a tough couple of years, and I've spent a lot of time away from home. I know everyone has sacrificed, not just me. However, I just got off the phone with the Naval Academy, and I'd like to go there next to work alongside my soon-to-be fiancée. She recently accepted a position as an instructor, and the Academy mentioned they have a couple of openings right now.*

Navy: *How about Norfolk? You could be an instructor there.*

Me: *Ummm... yeah, that's not really the same. As I just said though, there are spots available at the Naval Academy—I got off the phone with them like 10 minutes ago. Call them if you need to, I can give you the number. Can't you just let me go there?*

Navy: *Well, there are spots available—they're just not for you. How about San Diego?*

Me: *I don't think we're on the same page. Do you have anything in D.C.? It's close to Annapolis.*

Navy: *No.*

Me: *No? Seriously? You're telling me there isn't a single job for a Lieutenant in the entire, giant, five-sided building called the Pentagon? Nothing at the Navy Yard? Not even a base gym where I can hand out basketballs?*

Navy: *No, there isn't. How about this though...Would you consider putting your name in for an Admiral's aide position? You would have to interview.*

Me: *Yes.*

Navy: *Awesome. I have an opening in Guam, what do you think abou...*

Me: *..I seriously don't think you're listening to a wor...*

Navy: *...Wait, hold on. Something just popped up in D.C. I'll put your name in, but you'll need to be ready to move fast.*

Me: *Sure, put me in.*

———

I never thought I would get an interview. But one Saturday in October, while I was golfing with my Commanding Officer and a few junior officers at a course near our base in Point Mugu, the Skipper's cell phone rang as we were putting on the 10th green.

"Yes, Sir, he's right here, actually. Do you want to talk to him?" My Skipper looked at me, and I had no idea what was happening. He extended the phone to me and said, "The Admiral wants to talk to you."

And that's how my interview happened. It wasn't so much a Q&A session like a traditional interview; the Admiral really only asked me two things: 1) This job will involve a lot of work, and you'll have long hours with extensive travel. Are you really sure you want to do this? And 2) Could you be here after Thanksgiving?

I wasn't entirely sure what I was getting into, but I knew this opportunity would bring me closer to Eleanor, allowing us to finally start our lives together. So, I turned to my Skipper, covered the phone, and whispered, "Sir, he wants me to be there in a couple of weeks? Will that be ok?" I still had at least four months left in my squadron tour, but he nodded and gave his approval. So, I said "yes" to both of the Admiral's questions, finished the round, and then went home to start packing.

My parents and Pappy had flown out to spend Thanksgiving with me, and given the timing of the move, Pappy decided to join me on the cross-country drive. I had a blast, complete with a stop in Las Vegas where we gambled and wolfed down sushi, followed by Colorado Springs, where we visited Red Rocks and the Air Force Academy, and finally St. Louis, Missouri, where we toured Budweiser and took a ride to the top of the iconic Gateway Arch. The conversation flowed easily, and he listened intently as I recounted my recent experiences in Afghanistan.

One night, we were staying in a hotel near Busch Memorial Stadium when I woke up around 4 AM to the sound of him getting dressed.

"What's going on?" I asked, rubbing my eyes, wondering where he was planning to go.

"Nothing, just go back to sleep."

"What are you talking about? Where are you going?" I asked, sitting up in the bed beside his.

"I have to go to the ER, but I'll be back."

"What?! I'll drive you! What's wro—"

"Shut the f*ck up and go back to sleep. I'll be back in an hour."

I'd never heard him swear like that. I would have laughed if it weren't so serious. So, I did what he told me. He didn't have a cell phone, so I hoped he knew where the hotel was and how to get a taxi. Sure enough, a few hours later he was back, and we never spoke about it again. Whatever was troubling him that morning, he was definitely too embarrassed to talk about it with me.

Later that day, we drove to Columbus, Ohio, to stay with my brother for a couple of days before heading to Pennsylvania. I spent a couple days with my parents in Tatamy before heading down to Maryland to crash at Eleanor's apartment for a few weeks while we tried to figure out our next move.

At this point in my career, I was a cocky lieutenant, fresh from combat and convinced I knew how the Navy worked. As it turned out, working at the Navy International Programs Office was one of the best jobs I've had in uniform and opened my eyes to numerous opportunities outside the cockpit. I had the chance to travel the globe, often with my soon-to-be wife, while working alongside some incredibly talented people.

In fact, the experience was so fulfilling that my next first choice was to leave the Navy and explore new opportunities. But that was a conversation I would have with the Navy later. Today, I wasn't focused on my career or what came next—I was simply grateful for the phone call on a golf course that had brought me here, to stand at the altar. As I waited for Eleanor to walk down the aisle with her father, I realized that while the Navy had taken my career in unexpected directions, it had ultimately led me exactly where I needed to be—right here, ready to say "yes" again and marry the love of my life.

Perhaps the Navy was wiser than I ever realized.

CHAPTER 12
LEMOORE & MORE

Isaiah 43:16 *"I am the Lord, who opened a way through the waters, making a dry path through the sea."*

2004-2009

In 2004, when I accepted orders that would take us from D.C. to Lemoore, California, I don't think Eleanor was thrilled. Supportive, yes, as always, but not thrilled. I was about halfway through my tour as a Flag aide when it was time to decide on my career path. Though I was enjoying myself, I *really* didn't want to deploy anymore, and that's what I was facing next.

The typical career path after your first shore tour leads back to sea for what's known as a "disassociated sea tour," a 24 to 30-month assignment with a deployable unit, though not necessarily with an aviation squadron. This could involve serving on an Air Wing staff, being an officer assigned to ship's staff on an aircraft carrier, or, in some cases, working as a Training Officer, where graduates of specialized schools train others in a squadron.

And like I said, I didn't want to do any of that.

Me, 2004: *Okay, my time is almost up with this job in D.C., and I think I'm ready to leave the Navy. It's time to transition to civilian life, start a family, and begin a new career! Here is my official resignation letter…*

Navy: *WAIT! Don't do that. I know the last couple of years have been tough, but that's not typical at all. This whole Afghanistan situation will be resolved soon. Don't you enjoy flying? Isn't it incredible? We have openings for Air Wing staff positions—some in Oceana, Virginia, and others in Lemoore, California. Everyone wants Virginia, but there are currently three openings in Lemoore. You can choose whichever one you want, and you could start a family out there.*

Me: *Wait a second… Why doesn't anyone want to go to Lemoore?*

Navy: *………Don't worry about it. Just pick one.*

Me: *Okay, fine. One more tour, but that's it.*

Navy: *Excellent!*

Me: *Why do you sound like Mr. Burns? And stop steepling your fingers together, that just looks evil. I said I'd go.*

The timing of my move to California was quite favorable. I was joining an air wing and an aircraft carrier that were gearing up for deployment, which meant Eleanor could stay in Washington, D.C., and continue working in her new job. After her six-year career in the Navy, we decided together that it made more sense for her to leave while I stayed in. It's a constant challenge for military couples to be stationed together, especially when they belong to different communities within their branch of service. So, in early 2005, I packed up the car and headed west to join the Air Wing aboard the USS Abraham Lincoln for a deployment across the Pacific Ocean.

During that deployment, I got a crash course in coordinating operations between all of the squadrons and the ship team. As the only E-2C NFO in the group, I was surrounded by experts from every other type of aircraft. My roommate, whose call sign was "Suede," took me under his wing and showed me the ropes of being an effective staff officer in this new environment. I soaked up everything he had to teach me about Naval Aviation—though I was far less receptive to his repeated attempts to drag me to church.

Our desks were crammed into a small, two-man stateroom right under catapult #2. Headphones were essential during flight operations; when jets are launching, it's like having a jet engine in your living room. One day, while I zoned out listening to music, Suede tapped my shoulder. "Hey, Boo Boo (my call sign). If you're walking past a house and see someone drowning in a pool… what would you do?"

I pulled out my headphones, sighed, and asked, "What are we doing here? Is this a metaphor for something?"

"No, seriously, what would you do?" he pressed.

"Okay, I'll bite. I'd keep my headphones in and continue walking past the house. Because, maybe, just maybe, it's none of my business. Maybe they want to drown," I replied, my tone laced with sarcasm.

"Come on. Wouldn't you throw him a life preserver?" he pressed, trying to make his point.

This wasn't the first time Suede had tried to "save" my soul, and frankly, I was over it. On deployment, especially in aviation, we didn't keep a "normal" sleep schedule. It wasn't uncommon to be up until 3:00 AM and then sleep until well into the afternoon. So, on multiple Sundays, I'd be dead asleep, and without fail Suede would shake me awake, whispering, "Booooo Booooo. Wanna go to church with me?"

Usually, I'd mumble something like, "…no. But tell God I said hi," and roll over.

But this time, I had zero interest in his life-preserver analogy. I simply responded, "Sure. Whatever," and stuffed my headphones back into my ears.

When the deployment ended, I flew off the ship and returned to reunite with Eleanor, who had already been in California for a few weeks. As we landed in Lemoore and I stepped out of the cockpit, I finally understood what people meant about the heat in the Central Valley. At 110 degrees, it felt like stepping straight into a sauna. Apparently, this was considered a 'cool' day, since it had reached 120 just the day before. Still, I couldn't complain. Eleanor had managed the entire move to California on her own—finding a house, unpacking everything, and even putting away all my clothes so I wouldn't have to lift a finger when I got home. I have to give her credit for making it all look effortless.

As we settled into our new city as newlyweds, we began making friends within both the military and the local community. In late summer of 2006, I asked Eleanor if she would mind if I started coaching wrestling. I had been away from the wrestling room for a couple of years and was starting to get the itch. Earlier that afternoon, I took a chance and stopped by the wrestling room at one of the high schools in Hanford, CA. I knocked on the coach's door, introduced myself with a brief résumé, and asked if he needed any help in the room. He was a brand-new coach, fresh out of college, and he gladly accepted my offer.

Around the same time, we became fast friends with Crystal and Kenny, a military couple introduced to us by mutual friends. Kenny was in my Air Wing, and we hit it off right away. The first time we met was at a pool party, and the moment Eleanor and I walked in, we were both handed beer bongs. I knew right then that we'd made friends for life.

Life seemed to be moving quickly in those years. Not long after, our first son, Tyler, was born at the hospital on Naval Air Station Lemoore. Just a week later, Kenny and Crystal celebrated the birth of their first child in the very same room where Eleanor had delivered Tyler. It was a shared milestone that cemented our bond even further.

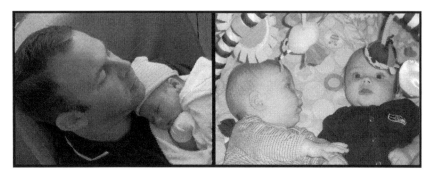

Left - Tyler on day 1. Right - Tyler and his new buddy getting to know each other

W hile we were living in Lemoore, I had the unique opportunity to become qualified in the F/A-18 Super Hornet. Not only was it an exhilarating airplane to fly, but it also provided me with a much broader perspective when I returned to the E-2C Hawkeye. Having firsthand experience in a fighter cockpit allowed me to better anticipate what the pilots and WSOs needed during missions. At the same time, I was able to share insights from the Hawkeye perspective with the aircrew I flew with in the F/A-18 community, bridging a gap between two very different worlds.

About a year into my tour, the Navy once again had plans that didn't align with mine. To my complete surprise, I was one of only two people in the Navy to be promoted to the rank of Lieutenant Commander a year early—a rare honor that took me completely off guard. This unexpected promotion accelerated my career milestones, shifting my trajectory in ways I hadn't anticipated. Shortly after, my record went in front of the Department Head screening board, and I was fortunate enough to be selected to return to the fleet.

In a squadron, department heads (or DHs) manage critical areas like maintenance, operations, admin, training, and safety. Career progression in these roles depends heavily on how you're ranked against your peers, with top marks being essential to staying on the path forward. But honestly, I never spent much time worrying about where I ranked or trying to get ahead. I just focused on flying, having fun, and living my best life.

When it came time to submit my preferences for the DH tour, I decided to shake things up and try something different. You know the drill by now...

Me, 2007: *Lemoore was awesome. How about we try Norfolk for the next squadron tour?*

Navy: *Nope, you're staying in California. Back to Point Mugu. And you should get there right now.*

Me: *But I just got here. Can't I ju—*

Navy: *Shhhhh...No more talking.*

Me: *Fine. I'll go. Just get your finger off my lips.*

So, in October of 2007, I returned to Point Mugu, where I joined a squadron gearing up for deployment. While I was there, I ran the Administrative Department for about a year, followed by the Maintenance Department for another year. I worked alongside a couple of my best friends, Chud and Party Boy (these are callsigns, not the names their mothers gave them). Chud and I were roommates in a two-man stateroom through two combat deployments, constantly encouraging and challenging each other to be better. We had countless late-night discussions about life, marriage, kids, and the Navy, and even after I left the squadron, we talked every few weeks. Party Boy and I went way back—he was the pilot I flew with on that Norfolk trip when I reunited with Eleanor. Years later, he would even serve as the guest speaker at my retirement ceremony.

Party Boy, Chud, and Me somewhere in the Pacific Ocean

While stationed at Point Mugu, Eleanor and I welcomed our second child, Travis, in 2009. I found out she was pregnant after returning from a month-long training exercise at sea, and she had managed to keep the news from me until I got back. This time, I was scheduled to be home for a few weeks before leaving again for a six-month deployment.

Eleanor and our 2-year-old son, Tyler, were there on base waiting for me at the "Fly-in," which is exactly what it sounds like: at the end of an underway period, all of the jets, planes, and helicopters launch from the carrier and return home. It's always a joyous event, and the longer you've been away, the larger the crowds and the longer the tears flow. But she didn't share the news in front of the hangar—she waited until later.

When we got home, there was a welcome home card sitting on the kitchen counter with a limerick inside. The limerick ended with something about looking in the oven. Curious, I opened the oven to find a sticky note with the number '11:27' on it and a single Hawaiian roll sitting on the rack.

I didn't get it. I wasn't expecting a riddle—I just wanted to take a shower and wash the smell of the ship off me.

"Roll on a rack?" I asked, a smile spreading across my face as I nodded. "Oh yeeeeaaaah." I wasn't sure what time Tyler's nap was, but I was already thinking of ways to distract him for 30 minutes. Ok, maybe five.

"No. Look again," she said. "What is that?"

".........wait...WHAT?"

It finally clicked. To be fair, a Hawaiian roll is not a bun. I would've gotten it if it were a hot dog bun, a hamburger bun, or even a sticky bun. Heck, even a picture of a woman's hair tied up in a bun. But I digress.

You probably figured this out right away, but she was trying to tell me that there was a bun in the oven. And he was due at the end of November. Hopefully, I'd be home in time for the birth.

We were very much in love, building a life together, writing our story —the four of us—and it felt great.

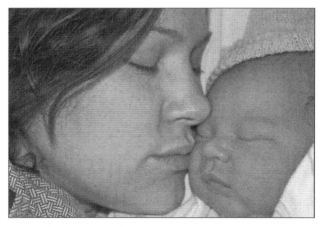

Eleanor and our 2nd son, Travis. Yes, I made it home in time!

CHAPTER 13
FIRST CHOICE!

Philippians 2:13 *"For God is working in you, giving you the desire and the power to do what pleases him."*

2009-2013

For the first time in my career, I received my first choice of assignments. It happened like this:

Me: *Can I go to Newport, Rhode Island?*

Navy: *Yes.*

In December 2009, less than a week after Travis was born, we were on the move again, heading to our new home. We spent the next year in Newport while I pursued a master's degree at the Naval War College. For the first time in our marriage, no deployments were looming on the horizon. We could finally settle into life as a married couple, syncing our routines, our plans, and our dreams—all while raising two kids.

It turns out, when you're a part-time husband and parent—never home for more than a few weeks at a time—and then suddenly, you start coming around every day with your dumb ideas about how things should work, there are some growing pains.

The only real fight we've ever had as a couple happened in Newport. Sure, we'd argued before, but this one was ugly. I don't even remember what triggered it, though it was probably me.

I was like the new guy at work who walks into a crowded meeting on his first day and says, "Hey, you're all stupid and doing things wrong. My way is better. Got it? Cool. I'm off to play golf. Bye."

The next morning, that same guy shows up to find his stuff packed in a suitcase in the lobby, and his badge doesn't work anymore.

Luckily, my fight with Eleanor didn't escalate to that level. I didn't have to leave—I just slept in another room for a night. By the next day, we were back to normal. But just as the dust was settling at home, my other boss—the Navy—came back with news about our next move.

Me, 2010: *Can I go to Tampa, Florida, for the next job? I've already arranged it with my future boss, and he says he'd love to have me.*

Navy: *Did you say Germany? It's time for you to work on a major staff, and I've got just the job for you.*

Me: *Yeah, I get the staff thing—it's what we all have to do at this point. But they have the same type of jobs in Florida. I've already talked to this guy, it's basically a done deal. You just need to type my name into the spreadsheet or whatever it is you do. D-U-E-L-L-E-Y. Like the truck, but with two Ls, and tw…*

Navy: *So you're interested in Germany?*

Me: Sigh. *Sure. Why not?*

Navy: *Excellent. Here are your orders to Germany, Lieutenant Commander Dually.*

That detour from Florida to Germany turned out to be incredible—no complaints at all. We lived in a small town outside Stuttgart, traveled all over Europe, attended countless festivals, and drank liters upon liters of beer. In my free time, I became an assistant wrestling coach at Patch High School, the Department of Defense school in the Stuttgart area.

By then, I was older, no longer in my wrestling prime, and recovery took longer. One incident during practice made me think my wrestling days might be over. I rolled my ankle during a match, feeling a sharp pain. I kept going because I wasn't about to let a high school kid see me tap out, but it hurt. After practice was over and everybody had left, I hopped out of the room on one leg, gingerly got in my car, and drove home using my left foot on the gas and brake. After two days of hobbling around, Eleanor convinced me to go to the ER and get it checked out.

After what felt like hours of waiting, imagining the worst—a break, a tear, something serious—the doctor finally walked out with my X-ray in hand. In the most German way possible, he bluntly told me in English, "There is nothing wrong with you. You can go home. Goodbye."

I walked out of that ER embarrassed. Actually, I was pissed at Eleanor for making me go, only to be told I was fine again. It made me start questioning whether I even knew what real pain was or if I just needed to suck it up. This wasn't the first time I felt dismissed, and it wouldn't be the last. In hindsight, it was just the start of a pattern that would unfold over the next few years.

But hospitals aren't always bad. In early 2013, we found out we were adding our third child to the family—another boy. During Eleanor's first ultrasound, the German doctor was moving the probe through the goop on her belly and casually blurted out, "Ah... there is penis. See?

"Yes, I see," I replied, glancing at Eleanor as our plan to wait and be surprised about the baby's gender was casually shattered.

But inside, I was shouting, *"YES!!! IT'S GOING TO BE A BOY!"* Boys are so much easier. They can pee wherever they want, they don't stress about emotions or feelings. They're tough—they wrestle, play football, do all the things I love. I'm just not cut out to play with dolls.

That ultrasound turned out to be the only glimpse we'd get of the baby's gender, as every subsequent scan showed him positioned in ways that conveniently hid the space between his legs. But I didn't need another look—I *knew* it was a boy.

So, in September 2013, when it was time for boy #3 to arrive, we checked into a German hospital in Stuttgart. The facility was excellent, the staff was fantastic, and thankfully, English was widely spoken because my German was limited to ordering beer and making dinner reservations.

Which is why, during labor, I was completely confused when one of the nurses announced, "Euer Mädchen ist hier."[1]

Wait, what? Who is here, the doctor? I know Mädchen means girl, but who are you talking about?

Then the nurse held up the baby, and we saw exactly what she meant. There she was—our precious, perfect little girl. I've never been more shocked in my life. It felt like the universe had played an elaborate trick on me—in the greatest way possible.

Adding to the irony of the moment, the nursing staff had, of course, laid out a blue blanket to wrap her in, fully prepared for a baby boy. So there she was, tiny and perfect, wrapped in a blue blanket—her first act of defying expectations.

When you're convinced you're having a boy, you make lists of boy names, gather boy clothes, and stock up on blue toys. Why would you have a backup plan for girl's stuff? So over the next two days, Eleanor and I sat in the hospital room, poring over baby name books while the staff kept pestering us to fill out the official paperwork. Meanwhile, Nora slept peacefully in the tiny blue onesies we'd packed, thinking she was going to be a boy. Finally, we settled on a name that felt like a miniature version of Eleanor: Nora.

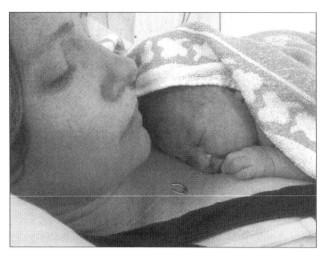

Surprise!

Our time in Germany was already incredible, and now, it had become unforgettable. For the first time, I learned what it was like to 'play with dolls.' I saw my daughter in a way I never expected, and it completely changed me.

And the good times kept rolling. During my tour in Germany, I was selected for Aviation Squadron Command—the pinnacle of a naval aviation career.

CHAPTER 14
COMMANDING MY LIFE

Revelation 3:17 *"You say, 'I am rich. I have everything I want. I don't need a thing!' And you don't realize that you are wretched and miserable and poor and blind and naked."*

2014-2017

W ithout a doubt, my time as a Commanding Officer was the most fun I had during my 24 years in the Navy. Getting there took 17 years of hard work, late nights, a ton of good luck and timing, and most importantly, the love and support of my family.

Like everyone who serves, I spent long stretches away from home during those 17 years—sometimes just a couple of weeks for training, other times six months or more for deployments. Each homecoming was a reminder of what truly mattered. Getting out of the plane and reuniting with my family lifted a weight I carried through every mission. And there were lots of them over the years, too many to count.

Homecomings are the best

Stepping into the role of "Skipper" (the mostly affectionate name for Commanding Officers) adds a new level of responsibility. As a Skipper, you're responsible not just for the mission but for the lives and careers of the men and women under your command. You are the leader, the strategist, the mentor—the one who sets the tone. The success or failure of every single action rests on your shoulders, and that's a burden you don't take lightly.

Of course, your decisions aren't made in isolation; they're shaped by years of experience, an intimate knowledge of your aircraft, and above all, deep trust in the people under your command. The weight of command is always present, making it a stressful yet fulfilling experience.

It's tough, demanding, and it'll test you in ways you never imagined, but there's nothing else like it. But no matter how much responsibility you carry on your shoulders, the job comes with rewards that are hard to put into words. You're not just leading; you're writing a chapter in Navy history, and that stays with you long after you've hung up your flight suit.

Before the change of command ceremony in 2016, I spent 14 months as the Executive Officer (XO), preparing for the role. But to understand how I got to this point, we need to rewind to 2014, when my family and I left Germany and returned to the States.

———

The move from Germany back to California in 2014 was uneventful—a blessing considering we were moving all our belongings across the world, including a newborn baby girl. Things appeared to be lining up perfectly for us.

This time, it was up to me to find a place to live. I flew out to California while the rest of the family stayed in Pennsylvania with my parents. After checking out a handful of rentals that were all just "meh," I stumbled upon a listing that had just hit the MLS. It was a huge place in Camarillo—the biggest house we'd ever lived in—close to the base and nestled in the heart of a newer neighborhood. Plus, I already knew a few friends who lived just a few blocks away. The landlord, a former Air Force pilot, and I hit it off right away during the tour. It instantly felt like we were meant to be in that house, which is exactly what I told Eleanor when I called her from my hotel room that night.

Settling in, we quickly became part of the community. Eleanor and I enrolled the kids in local schools and activities, gradually connecting with neighborhood families and military friends. We found a great preschool just a few blocks away and were able to enroll Travis and Nora soon after we settled in. The preschool was part of a Lutheran church in Camarillo, which initially gave us pause. My memories of going to church as a kid weren't great—I dreaded it—and Eleanor's experiences growing up were even more complicated. Neither of us was eager to send our kids to a religious school. Thankfully, the preschool focused on creating a safe, nurturing space without emphasizing religious teachings, which felt like the right fit for our family. At that stage, our priorities were pretty simple: 1) Are they safe? and 2) How much is this going to cost us?

A few months later, a neighborhood acquaintance, Mike, introduced me to a group called Adventure Guides, a father-child program run through the YMCA. Through Adventure Guides, I bonded with some of the other dads during overnight retreats, often gathering around a campfire long after the kids hunkered down in tents or cabins.

One of those conversations stuck with me. Mike was navigating a separation and impending divorce, and our talks often turned deep—especially for two guys sitting around a fire drinking bourbon. Those nights opened me up to the idea of spiritual growth in a way I hadn't explored before.

Around Christmastime, Nora's preschool class handed out flyers for an upcoming Christmas at the Barn service on a farm just a few minutes from our house. Nora was excited to see the animals, so we agreed to go.

As we turned off the main road, signs guided us down a dirt road to the back of the property. Outside the barn, white Christmas lights were strung up, while inside, benches and bales of hay were arranged before a makeshift stage. We settled onto the hay bales as the worship team began to play. Suddenly, I was overwhelmed with emotion, tears streaming down my face as the story of Jesus' birth unfolded before me. A thought kept echoing in my mind, insisting that I needed to believe and to change. Yet, I didn't know what that meant. Perhaps I was simply meant to start attending church?

A few days later, I mentioned the idea of finding a church home to Eleanor, but life intervened, and we dropped the topic. After all, life was wonderful. I felt fantastic. I was on top of the world.

Christmas at the Barn

PART THREE
BREAKING DOWN

Ecclesiastes 3:1 "For everything there is a season,
a time for every activity under heaven."

CHAPTER 15
THE ELEPHANT IN THE ROOM IS ON MY CHEST

Proverbs 17:22 *"A cheerful heart is good medicine, but a broken spirit saps a person's strength."*

Friday, July 31, 2015. 4:15 PM

On a clear and sunny summer afternoon in Camarillo, California, my friend and flight surgeon Dr. Seth walked with me through the emergency room doors. I was having chest pains, and as much as I tried, I couldn't suck it up anymore. It was the first outward, physical sign that something was wrong.

At that time, I was a seasoned Naval Officer, 17 years into my Navy career. I served as the Executive Officer in an E-2C Hawkeye squadron —the Navy's carrier-based command and control workhorses, humming along since the Vietnam era.

I, too, believed I was a workhorse and that my life was humming along.

The chest pains had crept in a few months earlier, subtle at first. Despite being in decent shape – hitting the gym regularly and fueling myself with (mostly) healthy food for a 39-year-old—these crushing attacks would come out of nowhere every couple of weeks.

It felt as if someone had airlifted an elephant onto my chest, squeezing the air from my lungs and blurring the world around me. All I could do was sit there, ride it out, and hope nobody noticed the grimace on my face. Public settings, like squadron briefings, were the worst. Here I was, the leader, and my body had chosen to stage a mutiny.

One such mutiny unfolded just before my turn to address the 170+ sailors and officers in my squadron. I was sitting next to the senior enlisted advisor in the front row, and I stared at my boots so he wouldn't notice, waiting for normalcy to return. It did, and I stood up, walked to the front of the small auditorium, and tried to act like nothing had happened.

A week later, I mentioned these attacks to Dr. Seth, our base flight surgeon, while we sat on a sofa in my office discussing various medical issues throughout the command. As I was telling him about my ongoing problems, the familiar weight once again slammed onto my chest. I stopped mid-sentence, clasped my hands together, and stared at my flight boots once more as the moment passed.

"Is it happening now?" he asked, his voice laced with concern. My shaky nod was all the answer he needed. "Why don't we go get you checked out," he declared more than asked.

We hopped in his car, and he drove to the emergency room. On the way, I sent off a quick text to my wife. "Hey, I'm going with Seth to see a doc in Camarillo...just getting checked out for something." I tried to downplay the whole thing, but of course, she went into full-blown panic mode.

"What's going on?" she asked.

"It's nothing, just having some pains in my chest."

"WHAT?! I'll meet you there; just give me five minutes," she texted.

I almost channeled my inner Pappy and yelled "SHUT THE F UP AND GO BACK TO SLEEP, I'LL BE BACK IN AN HOUR!" But that would have been insane. So I tried to take a deep breath, and responded "It's okay; just stay with the kids. I'm going to get a couple of tests, and then Seth can drop me off at home." With three kids under the age of nine, someone needed to stay with them.

The ER lobby consisted of the usual collection of ailments, with people scattered on uncomfortable plastic seats while they waited to be called back. And here we were, two thirty-something-year-old men in green flight suits, a sight that probably turned a few heads in the waiting room.

"Great, this is going to take hours," I thought, looking around at a bunch of people that needed to stop coughing, suck it up, and go home.

We walked up to the front desk, and I greeted the triage nurse behind the counter. She smiled, and said, "We don't see pilots in here all that often, how can I help you guys?" Her demeanor instantly changed when Dr. Seth said, "My friend here is having chest pains, and I need to get him evaluated."

I was quickly whisked away in a wheelchair, hooked up to an EKG, blood was drawn, and I answered a barrage of questions.

At some point my friend Mike stopped by the hospital, prompted by Eleanor's frantic call. I learned later that she had called his wife to see if somebody could watch the kids. Mike's wife had texted him, and because he was across the street from the hospital at the time, he told Eleanor he would pop in to see if it was something serious. It was a blessing to have Mike there, as he had recently suffered a heart attack and was familiar with what I was going through.

After an hour or so of waiting, one of the doctors walked in with a clipboard containing all the test results and gave me the verdict: a clean bill of health. "It's most likely stress," he said. "You're in a very difficult line of work, and you have a lot going on in your life with a lot of responsibilities. I would recommend relaxing for a week and taking some time to yourself."

"Oh. That's great." I said, not really meaning it. I mean, it was great news that I wasn't dying, but it still left a hollow feeling in my gut. I craved a diagnosis, a pill, a treatment plan, something tangible to explain these attacks. Because in my mind, stress was for the weak, and I was far from that. So, I walked out, gingerly, feeling stupid. *"Why even speak up?"* I thought to myself. *"Just suck it up, and stop being weak."*

That night, I lay in bed and cried as I faced the window, unable to let my wife see the tears. Because I had something wrong with me. And nobody believed me. And I couldn't fix it.

The attacks continued. Sometimes I would go for weeks or even months between the giant elephant showing up. But he always came back.

It was a long eight years before I discovered the real cause.

CHAPTER 16
A FRIEND'S CONCERN

Proverbs 14:29 *"People with understanding control their anger; a hot temper shows great foolishness."*

Wednesday, February 9, 2022. 10:15 AM

T he day I inexplicably snapped at a coworker—41 years after my infamous kindergarten pants-wetting incident—was a new low. I'd lost my temper over something so trivial, and I was in such a rage that I can't even remember the exact details of what was said. I just knew that I was in an awful mood, I hadn't slept in forever, and poor Edward, seated across the conference table, took the brunt of my frustrations after he complained about something that seemed completely ridiculous at the time.

It was winter of 2022, about five years since my Command tour in California, and I was now a Captain in Washington, DC, leading teams of subject matter experts tasked with assessing critical infrastructure across the Department of Defense. After the incident, I was in my office when Kurt, one of my team members, stopped in the doorway to chat. Kurt, a retired Air Force cyber expert with Philly roots, was a big guy. I trusted his judgment in the field and valued his takes on the Eagles and Phillies. But instead of his usual Philly rant, he hit me with a direct question:

"You okay, Captain?" he asked, leaning against the door.

"What? Yeah, why?" I replied, trying to play it off.

"You kinda lost it back there. And… I gotta say, Sir, you look like a bag of dicks," he said bluntly.

"Thaaaanks, man," I shot back, my tone drenched in sarcasm.

"I'm serious. Are you sleeping alright?" he pressed.

I was surprised. No one had ever asked about my well-being so directly. "Well…" I trailed off, unsure how much to share about the sleepless nights that had become routine.

"Not really," I admitted quietly after a moment.

"You should talk to someone," Kurt said, meeting my eyes.

"Why? Because I'm 'tired'? Because I'm angry?" I scoffed, mocking him with air quotes.

"Exactly. Because something's off, and there are people who can help," Kurt insisted, easing into the chair across from me. "Look, man, I was in a special forces unit years ago…"

THE DC SLIDE

As I listened to Kurt tell his story, I thought back to how I had gotten here. My command tour was over, I had a couple more deployments under my belt, and tons more time away from home. Our move from sunny Southern California to the hectic pace of Northern Virginia in 2017 was all because of a new assignment at the Pentagon—a place both respected and dreaded. Once word got out that I was eyeing a specific job at the Pentagon, my path felt set—like cattle being funneled into a chute.

So, in March of 2017, I had new orders in hand, and Eleanor and I started our usual routine of house hunting. After six moves in twelve years, we started to feel like seasoned professionals. Our realtor in Virginia, Lori, was an absolute blessing, spending an entire week driving us all over the DC metro area, but the market was so tough that our first trip didn't turn up anything. We still needed a place to live, so Eleanor, ever determined, went back a few weeks later with a new list of homes to check out. Thankfully, their persistence paid off, and the stars aligned; we found a new home and settled in, planning to stay for about two years—ready for whatever the Navy threw at us next.

Military life often comes with a built-in community through your squadron or unit, and over the years, we've been lucky enough to make great friends wherever we've landed. And in Northern Virginia, we found ourselves in an amazing neighborhood where the friend-ships ran deep and felt like they'd last. Our kids thrived, diving into sports and activities that only strengthened our ties to the community.

Things took a significant turn at the end of 2017 when I was faced with a major career decision. Just before Thanksgiving, I received a phone call from the head of Naval Aviation, congratulating me on my selec-tion for the prestigious "Nuclear Power Pipeline." This program is the rigorous training path that qualifies officers to command nuclear-powered aircraft carriers—an opportunity that leads to Major Command at Sea and a path for promotion to Admiral. To put it in perspective, more astronauts have flown in space than officers who have commanded one of the Navy's eleven aircraft carriers.

I had about 24 hours to decide the next 10+ years of my career. This path wasn't one I had desired, as there were other command opportu-nities available; however, now that it was actually within my reach I had to make a decision. If I turned it down, there would be no more opportunities for me. But if I accepted, it was going to be a long and winding road, filled with late nights and lots of time spent away from home.

I thought back to the guidelines of pain versus reward. The rewards of accepting would be fantastic: what's better than commanding a floating city, a mobile airfield, and a crew of 5,000+ people depending on your leadership?

What mattered most to me were the four people in my house who also depended on me. I couldn't bear the thought of leaving them behind for one more week in their lives, let alone for months at a time. I couldn't stand to watch Eleanor pick up all the pieces of our life and move again or leave her sitting alone at another baseball game or wrestling match, wondering if I would ever come home.

Although she said all the right words, telling me, "I'll support whatever you want to do," I knew in her heart that she didn't mean it. And in my own heart, I didn't want it either.

So, I said no.

It crushed me to have to make that decision. In 24 hours, I went from thinking my career was on track to realizing that I was "persona non grata" in my aviation community. I felt pretty bitter for a long time. The blow to my ego was immense, and I felt like a part of my identity had suddenly been ripped away. I know it might sound like I'm holding a grudge, but I understood that it was just how the system worked, and I knew the game I was playing. As much as it stung, I boxed up those feelings, locked the lid tight, and pretended I didn't care…or at least I tried to.

Over the next few years, the signs of struggle got worse, I just didn't recognize it. Or maybe I did and simply ignored them.

I continued coaching, which helped me feel more connected to the community and more at home. Yet, something still felt off. Mood swings became the norm, swinging between highs and lows. One day, I'd be a great parent; the next, I'd be screaming at the kids for something as small as not putting their shoes away. Not just raising my voice, but *screaming*. On some level, I knew my temper was on a short fuse, and I understood the need to keep it in check at work or in public, where people might see me as an a$$hole. But at home, there was no one to judge me.

For seven years the elephant never left my side, jumping onto my chest when I least expected it. Dizzy spells accompanied by shortness of breath put me on my butt more times than I can remember, but I was afraid to say anything for fear of being embarrassed one more time when it turned out to be nothing. So, I did what I always did—I buried it and kept going.

One morning, I woke up with a pain in my throat. It wasn't so much a sore throat; it felt more like discomfort on the side of my windpipe. I couldn't swallow without experiencing serious pain. For the first week or so, I chalked it up to COVID or a virus. My body would fight it off like it always had. However, as weeks turned into months, I started to feel a little nervous. Maybe this was something more serious, like cancer or a problem with my thyroid. So, I made a doctor's appointment and underwent a full set of tests to eliminate my worst fears. But there was nothing there. Once again, I walked out the double doors with a wave goodbye and an orange bottle full of Motrin tablets.

There was another ER visit in the summer of 2021. Throughout the day, I began to feel some shortness of breath. Have you ever had that feeling after swimming all day, when you can't take a deep breath? That's what it felt like, except I hadn't gone swimming, and I spent most of the day lying on the sofa watching TV. In the early evening, Eleanor and I were walking our two dogs when I suddenly felt a stabbing pain shoot through both lungs. I sat down on a bench along the trail behind our house, trying to regulate my breathing. Each breath only intensified the stabbing pain. Through shallow breaths, I asked her to drive me to the base hospital.

It took us about 20 minutes to get there, and she couldn't drive fast enough for me. *"I should have called an ambulance,"* I thought. We arrived at an empty waiting room and were told that she would have to wait outside (this was in the heart of COVID). Eleanor obviously didn't want to leave my side, but her only option was to wait in the car in the parking lot. It was getting late, almost 9 PM by then, and there wasn't much she could do anyway.

I told her it would be okay. "Go home, I'll call you when I know something." I checked myself in and went through the drill all over again.

I lay motionless in the emergency room bed, waiting for results. Moving was difficult, as the slightest change in position brought sharp, stabbing pain to my chest. At first, I waved off any painkillers because… you know, that's for the weak. But when turning my head or blinking too quickly made the pain spike to a 10, I buckled and begged the nurse for a shot to make it go away.

Much like my experience in Camarillo a few years earlier, I was released at 12:30 AM with a clean bill of health and given some over-the-counter meds to add to the collection.

Since I was alone in the hospital without a car and it was well past midnight, I shuffled the 1.2 miles to the gate to hail an Uber. It was a military base, closed off to the outside world, there weren't taxis just hanging around. I didn't want to wake Eleanor or ask her to leave my kids home alone, and I certainly couldn't ask a neighbor for a ride when there was nothing wrong with me. So, I walked. Then sat to catch my breath. Then walked. Then sat again. All in the middle of a thunderstorm. Rain poured down on me, and I felt like lying down in the grass, staring up at the falling drops, just letting it wash over me. I kept gripping my chest, hoping the pain wouldn't buckle my knees.

I couldn't sleep that night—or most nights, for that matter. It had been years since I'd last had a full night of uninterrupted rest.

Most nights, I'd wake up every two hours or so. Sometimes, I'd fall back asleep. Other times, I wouldn't.

Some nights, I'd walk downstairs and flip on Netflix, hoping to escape my racing thoughts.

That rarely worked.

Some nights, I'd pour bourbon into a glass to see if that would help.

It didn't.

I tried to hide everything. Every feeling. Every ounce of fatigue. Every dirty bourbon glass. Every tear that betrayed me, silently sliding down my cheeks as I sat alone in the dark.

And all the repeated trips to the ER or doctor over the years led to nothing. There was absolutely nothing wrong with me. Every visit ended in an embarrassing trudge out of the hospital and back to my everyday life. I began to doubt my toughness and my tolerance for pain, wondering just how bad it had to be before a real problem existed.

I was a Captain in the Navy, a husband, a father, and a coach. I was expected to be strong, to lead, to inspire. And outwardly, I did all that. But behind the facade, I was crumbling.

Suck it up, Buttercup. There's no crying in Virginia.

RETURN TO THE OFFICE

So here I was back in 2022, just me and Kurt in my office. He had long ago taken a seat and closed the door as if this were my own personal counseling session, and I'd been listening to him recount his experiences for the past 30 minutes.

"So I knew when you lost it back there, that something was going on. And it's ok to admit that you need some help," Kurt continued.

His words hung in the air. It was an unexpected moment of vulnerability, especially between men, and a rare glimpse into someone else who quietly carrying a hidden weight on his shoulders.

The truth was, I was drowning in a sea of exhaustion. The weight of the world seemed to rest entirely on my shoulders for no reason whatsoever, and I was starting to buckle under the pressure.

"If you're sick, you see a doctor," Kurt said. "If your teeth hurt, you see a dentist, right? So if your mind needs help, why wouldn't you see a professional?"

What I didn't tell Kurt was that I had already sought medical help. I couldn't admit it to him because I was still embarrassed, still trying to keep my vulnerability and struggles hidden.

By this point, sleep deprivation had reached a crisis, and it couldn't have come at a worse time. In a few weeks I would be leading a team of civilians, contractors, and military personnel on a two-week mission to Rota, Spain, where we'd be working at the naval base. The mere thought of a sleepless transatlantic flight followed by executing tasks while jet-lagged sent waves of panic through me.

I was so desperate for relief that I went to the base medical center, hoping to find something to help. I told the corpsman I needed a sleep aid for the flight and to combat jet lag, which was only a half-truth, masking the deeper issue. When the doctor came in, she read the notes and stuck to basic questions, and I was relieved I didn't have to get into the real problem because my voice was already starting to crack as I answered.

As she typed notes into my file and wrote the prescription, I couldn't hold it back anymore. A single tear rolled down my face, but I wiped it away before she saw it.

Still, Kurt's suggestion to seek help had been a lifeline, and I followed through. It was time to face my demons and confront the elephant that refused to leave me alone.

.

CHAPTER 17
MISSING THE LIFELINE

Matthew 14:30-31 *"But when he saw the wind, he was afraid and, beginning to sink, cried out, 'Lord, save me!' Immediately Jesus reached out his hand and caught him. 'You of little faith,' he said, 'why did you doubt?'"*

Wednesday, March 16, 2022. 9:30 AM

A few weeks later, I sat in the waiting room of the behavioral health clinic, laptop in hand as I filled out screen after screen after screen of background information. I must have entered my name, address, and phone number over 500 times. I long for the day when you can provide personal information just once, have it stored in a database, and then allow any provider in the world to access it with your permission. Maybe that's a topic for another book.

Although I filled out all the information truthfully, as I sat across from the provider, I tried to present myself as a confident, healthy Naval Officer—one who didn't need anyone's help. Remember, I was still in uniform, conditioned my entire life to guard my personal issues closely. On top of that, the old mantra echoed in my mind: "Suck it up. Suck it up."

I shared as much as I could handle, trying to be honest about what was going on: racing thoughts about my future, sleepless nights, and drinking a few times a week. I had to be careful talking about some of this stuff, out of a perceived fear of my command finding out about what was going on, or maybe even getting pulled from my job and losing my security clearance.

She scribbled notes the whole time, barely making eye contact as I spoke.

Near the end of our session, she finally looked at me and said, "You're just dealing with normal stress, especially with retirement coming up. Once that's behind you, things should calm down. I'll write you a prescription to help you sleep better."

What? This is normal?

She kept talking, but I tuned her out. As the session ended, I shuffled out of yet another provider's office, feeling like an idiot.

I wasn't sure what I had been expecting—it was my first time seeing a mental health provider—but I knew medication wasn't the answer. Still, for some reason, I went to the pharmacy and picked up the meds, only to toss them in the trash when I got home.

Even though no one said it outright, I didn't need anyone hinting that I should just "suck it up."

Frustrated, disillusioned, and angry at the system, I swore I'd never go back.

"When's your next appointment?" Eleanor asked when I got home.

"I'm not going back."

"Why not?" she asked, concerned.

I told her about throwing away the meds and what the provider had said.

"Oh, honey, I'm so sorry. It's not supposed to be like this. That just wasn't the right person for you. Let's find someone else—even if we have to pay out of pocket."

Call me cheap, but I hate paying out of pocket for things that should already be covered by something I'm paying into. For the next few days, I hesitated to do anything at all. Honestly, it felt easier to ignore it and hope it would go away—like that random lump you find on your scalp and convince yourself it's probably nothing.

Once I worked up the nerve to start the process again, I made some calls, hoping to find a provider who wouldn't just try to pump me full of meds. Six weeks later (yes, SIX WEEKS), I found myself in another waiting room, filling out the same forms on yet another laptop. And yes, both clinics were using the same shared electronic health system.

"Mr. Doo-EL-ee?" The doctor stepped into the waiting room, glancing between me and the man seated across from me, waiting to see who would answer. People often struggle with my last name.

"Yes, that's me," I replied, following her through the open door and down the hall. "It's 'DUEL-ee,' like the truck," I added as I took a seat on the sofa across from her desk.

She introduced herself and asked why I had come to see her. I recounted the events of the past couple of years, all the while wondering if the laptop I'd been using in the waiting room was connected to the internet, or just sending 1's and 0's into the trash.

The doctor sat in front of her computer, staring at the screen and nodding as I spoke. The short, sharp clicking of the keyboard filled the silence between my responses.

"Are you married?"

"Yes, I'm married. We've been together for almost 18 years."

Clickety-click, clickety-click, clack.

My frustration bubbled beneath the surface as I tried my best to calm myself and answer her.

"Do you have any children?"

"Yes, three," I replied. *Shouldn't that be right there in my file, lady?*

Clickety-click, clickety-click, clack.

"Boys? Girls"

"YES, I'M MARRIED!!! YES, I HAVE THREE CHILDREN!!!" I wanted to scream. *"TWO BOYS, AND ONE GIRL!! WELL, WE THOUGHT WE WERE HAVING A 3RD BOY, BUT…..NEVER MIND!!!* "IT'S ALL IN THE F'ING FILE I JUST FILLED OUT!"

So, this session wasn't going well for me. It dragged on for about 45 minutes, even though it had taken me less than 15 minutes to fill out all the information in the waiting room. I don't think we discussed anything meaningful—just a word-for-word recap of my file, and a brief overview about the steps for scheduling more sessions.

I felt like I had wasted another morning chasing a solution, leaving me doubtful that I would return. Eleanor encouraged me to keep going, and eight days later, I found myself in the waiting room again, the same laptop in hand as I updated my answers to the same questions.

"Mr. Doo-EL-ee?" Another mispronunciation. Same walk to her office. Same sofa. Same review of the basic information, as if I'd gotten a divorce and added two more children to my life in the past week. This time, though, it only took 25 minutes to review the questions. So that was a plus.

She asked what I liked to do to relieve stress, but I didn't have a clear answer. "Golf, I guess. But that can add stress too." My joke fell flat as she continued typing away on her keyboard, never taking her eyes off the screen in front of her.

Clickety-click, clickety-click, clack.

"Do you take walks?" she asked.

"Yes," I replied. "My wife and I usually walk the dogs twice a day."

Clickety-click, clack.

"What about baths? Do you enjoy bubble baths?"

"ARE YOU KIDDING ME?" I screamed inside my head. *"Fuck this place."* It took every ounce of self-control to remain seated. I don't even remember if I answered her questions—it's probably in my file some-

where. All I wanted to do was stand up, smash the keyboard into a million pieces, and walk out.

But I didn't. I finished the session and let her schedule the next one for me, knowing deep down that I wasn't going to return. I wasn't ready to open up the boxes. I didn't have the patience, the tools, or even the awareness that they were the root of the problem. I felt scared. I had no faith in the process, no faith in myself, and I didn't know where to turn anymore.

CHAPTER 18
AAAAAAAAND, GO!

Deuteronomy 31:8 *"Do not be afraid or discouraged, for the Lord will personally go ahead of you. He will be with you; he will neither fail you nor abandon you."*

Wednesday, July 27, 2022. Around 9 AM

So after deciding that seeing a counselor wasn't in the cards, I pretended that it didn't matter anyway and threw myself into what was right in front of me: retiring from the Navy and transitioning into civilian life.

The Navy does a reasonably good job of preparing you for the transition. Everyone, whether they've served for 24 months or 24 years, must attend transition classes where they're hit with a whirlwind of information—from applying for Veteran's benefits to advice on what to wear to an interview. In the end, two key things stuck with me: 1) There are a ton of resources available to help, from websites and books to nonprofits that specialize in résumé writing and interview prep. And 2) leaving the only thing you've known for the last 2+ decades is, well, kinda stressful.

I get it—I'm not the first person to hang up the uniform and step into the civilian world. Millions before me have done it, and millions after me will, too. But I struggled. The more books I read and the more one-on-one sessions I attended, the more confused I became about my next step. Everyone told me I needed to be laser-focused on my goal. Otherwise, it was like throwing darts at a wall while blindfolded. I felt "dumb" for not being able to hop on a networking call and confidently say, "I'm seeking a role in the tech sector, and I want to specialize in manufacturing Bluetooth-enabled toaster ovens, but only silver ones."

I went through a few interviews, but none of them really grabbed me. I made it through three rounds of interviews with a large, well-known package delivery company and accepted a corporate role near DC. The salary wasn't what I hoped for, and I wasn't particularly excited about the job itself, but since it was the only offer I had at the time I said yes.

Around the same time, I was also engaged in some interesting conversations with a major US bank, but I wasn't sure it was going to lead to anything. But soon after I accepted the big giant package delivery company role, I received a verbal offer from the big bank, with the understanding that I could either work out of the DC office or relocate to Dallas. Moving from Virginia hadn't even crossed our minds, but after a few nights of discussion, we started to consider that a change of scenery might be good for us. At the hiring manager's suggestion, Eleanor and I eagerly booked a flight to Dallas to spend a few days exploring the area.

As a diehard Philly guy, I wanted nothing to do with Texas—especially not Dallas. I had visited Austin a couple of times and had been to Fort Worth once, about 20 years ago. When I pictured Dallas, my thoughts always went back to the TV show, or movies like *Friday Night Lights*. I imagined cowboy hats, dusty boots, and, of course, people decked out in Dallas Cowboys gear.

I was wrong.

The first thing we noticed was the infrastructure. Imagine, for just a second, a place where civil engineers have a blank canvas to design roads, bridges, and U-turn lanes along frontage roads under highways, where you never have to cross in front of traffic. Picture miles and miles of on-ramps where you don't need to be an experienced drag racer to accelerate from a cold start to highway speeds. It's nothing short of magical. Unlike the roads in Washington, D.C., which seem designed to confuse invaders (that's totally not true), or the freeway on-ramps in Southern California that give you only 10 to 20 feet to accelerate from 0 to 75 (that's totally true), the Dallas suburbs were designed to welcome in drivers like me.

Then there was the opportunity—not just for a job, but also for schools, sports, and culture. Conveniently, my parents had moved from Tatamy to Austin a few years ago, and my brother was in the Austin area as well, so the family would be a short drive away. As we drove through the neighborhoods that weekend, Eleanor and I already felt at home.

The only hurdle was the Dallas Cowboys, but I figured I could live with that. When the big bank extended a generous offer, I emailed the large global package delivery company to tell them I was out, and we began preparing for the move. Instead of staying in Virginia after retirement, where we had friends, neighbors, and a life we loved, we were moving to Texas—the land of Friday night lights, BBQ, country music, and cowboy boots (nah, those are just stereotypes. Well, except the football part, that's a real thing).

So now, we had to find a house—and quickly.

On Wednesday, July 27th, around 9 AM, Eleanor and I sat at our kitchen table in Virginia, flipping through rental listings. After our weekend visit to Texas we both knew the city and school district we wanted to focus on, and we were racing against the clock to get there in time for the first day of school on August 10th. We weren't ready to buy yet, so we planned to find a one-year rental before making a more permanent decision.

"Here. How about this one?" I turned my computer to show her what I'd found. "The elementary school is good, the neighborhood looks nice, and the price is just right."

"Yeah, I like that one. I'll call the realtor," Eleanor said, picking up her phone to dial the number from the listing.

As I continued searching, I overheard her side of the conversation: "Hi, my name is Eleanor, and I'm calling about a rental property." I heard her give the address, then after a few seconds heard "Oh, it's not available?… Okay… Yes… How much?… That sounds great."

"What sounds great?" I asked as she hung up.

"That was Cindy, the agent. The house isn't available, but she knows of another one in the same neighborhood. She'll text me the details."

A few minutes later, her phone pinged, and we checked the listing. "Perfect, that works. Let's call her back," I said, calling her on speakerphone.

Cindy answered on the first ring, her voice carrying a friendly Texas drawl. We asked a few questions about the lease, and she responded, "How about we meet there today to take a look at the house?"

"Well," I said, "we're in Virginia and won't be in Texas for about a week. But we need a place to live when we arrive, and we need an address to register our kids for school—sooner rather than later."

"Ah, no problem. How about I head over there now, and we can do a video chat? Will that work?" Cindy called us back about 15 minutes later, after she had opened the house and turned on all the lights. "Here's the master bedroom… And this is the living room," she said, panning the camera.

"Does it look like the pictures? And does it smell in there? Like cats or anything?" I asked. That was my main concern.

"Nope, no smell," she replied with a chuckle.

By 8 PM, we had signed the lease—the first time we'd ever agreed to live in a place without seeing it in person. And over the next 72 hours, we had a long to-do list: contact Lori, the real estate agent we'd worked with before to list our Virginia house for sale, pack everything we could fit into two vehicles, register the kids at their new schools, cancel Eleanor's clients for the next couple of weeks, forward our mail to Texas, turn off utilities in Virginia, turn on utilities in Texas, arrange for temporary furniture in Texas, pack clothes for 105-degree weather, pack clothes for 40-degree weather, bring business attire for work, find dog-friendly hotels for the drive, text friends along the route to see if we could meet up, get the oil changed in both vehicles since I'd forgotten to do it in the last couple of weeks, unregister the kids from their fall sports in Virginia, register them for fall sports in Texas, schedule movers for late August or September, fill out HR paperwork for my new job, change our military retirement paperwork to reflect the new address, update our auto insurance to Texas, and tell all of our friends in Virginia that we were moving….On Saturday….In like three days.

That night, we texted our Virginia friends and invited everybody to meet up at a nearby brewery on Friday so we could say our goodbyes. Despite everything we had to do, we pulled it off. It was hectic, but the Navy had prepared us. We made lists, assigned tasks to each other, and methodically checked things off in preparation for a Saturday morning departure. The drive down was enjoyable—we stopped in a few places and visited friends we hadn't seen in years, staying with some and having lunch with others. And we were excited to start over in a new city, with new adventures ahead.

The fall of 2022 brought new challenges. Starting a new job was familiar after countless Navy assignments, but this time I wasn't in my Naval Officer uniform—I was in corporate attire, with a badge around my neck. I was in a cyber management role, yet I lacked experience in the technical aspects of the job, and imposter syndrome hit hard. Most of my team was scattered across different corporate offices worldwide, so I hardly knew anyone locally. At home, I was a stranger in the neighborhood. At soccer games, football matches, and wrestling meets, I sat alone, surrounded by people who had been lifelong friends. When filling out emergency contact cards, the only people I could list were my parents, who lived over three hours away.

This isn't a "woe is me" story—everyone goes through this. But I was already stuffing my anxiety into that emotional box, just like I always had. The difference now was I no longer had outlets or distractions. Before, I had friends to golf with or grab beers with. I had coworkers to joke around with or vent to. I had neighbors to hang with during culdesac parties or pick up our mail if we were out of town. I had fellow coaches, and we'd spend Sunday nights after wrestling tournaments comparing notes and planning for the week ahead. I had purpose in my work, and people who seemed to need my leadership and expertise.

Then, all of that disappeared. My friends weren't here. My new coworkers didn't speak my language, and I didn't understand theirs. I didn't know a single neighbor.

I had no purpose.

There were people all around me, everywhere I turned. I was on video calls with my team at work all day, every day. Friends were just a phone call away. I spent time with my kids, attending all their events and activities. My wife slept inches from me, with two dogs constantly vying for their space.

Yet despite all this, I felt utterly alone.

CHAPTER 19
THE WEDDING BREAKDOWN

Psalm 42:11 *"Why am I discouraged? Why is my heart so sad?"*

Saturday, December 31, 2022. 4:15 PM

O n New Year's Eve 2022, just five months after we moved to Texas, I experienced a mental breakdown I never thought possible. I always believed that meltdowns happened only in the face of unimaginable tragedies—something so catastrophic it broke you. Otherwise, there was no excuse. You should be able to pull yourself together and "suck it up"—unless, of course, you were weak. At least, that's what I thought before it happened to me.

My brother, Bryan, was marrying the love of his life, and our entire extended family had gathered in Austin, Texas, to celebrate not only the New Year but the blending of two beautiful families. It was a weekend filled with promise and joy.

My family of five—Eleanor, Tyler, Travis, Nora, and me—had made the four-hour drive from the Dallas suburbs the day before. We left the dogs with a pet sitter, packed up the trusty minivan, and hit the road Friday morning, ready for a fun-filled weekend.

This trip also gave me a rare chance to reconnect with my aunts, uncles, and cousins. While I'd seen some of them earlier that year at my Navy retirement ceremony, for many, the last time we were all together was at Pappy's funeral back in 2020. The memories of that day, filled with both sorrow and shared love, lingered heavily in my mind all weekend.

Everyone was staying at the same hotel in Bee Cave on Friday night, with some of us planning to move over to the resort on Saturday morning for the wedding that evening. We arrived late Friday afternoon, dropped off our bags in the room, and headed straight to the rooftop bar to see who was there. Hotel bars have some weird gravitational effect on my family that NASA should probably study.

As the sun dipped lower over the hotel, it was time to head to the rehearsal dinner. We piled into Ubers and made our way to a casual gathering at a local steakhouse in Bee Cave. It was your typical rehearsal cocktail party—mingling with guests we hadn't met yet, catching up with old friends, and enjoying the lively atmosphere. Reconnecting with everyone should have felt grounding, like a lifeline, but instead, it had the opposite effect.

I was ready to tie one on that night. With no need to drive and my parents handling the kids, it seemed like the perfect opportunity to relax and unwind. It had been a tough couple of months—honestly, a tough few years. But for reasons I couldn't explain, I stopped after one beer and switched to tonic water early on. Something felt off, though I couldn't put my finger on what it was. I wasn't sick, and I didn't have a headache—I just didn't feel like drinking.

So instead, I spent the evening shuffling between different groups—some family, others people I was meeting for the first time. I laughed at their jokes and friendly teasing, answering the same questions over and over, trying to blend into the background.

"Yep, we just moved a few months ago. We love it here in Texas."

"No, I'm not carrying a gun. But I'm buying a cowboy hat next week to fit in better."

"Yes, there are a lot of people who move here from California. Haha. Don't California MY Texas!" We technically fit that stereotype, having lived in California multiple times.

If you look at any pictures from that night, you'll see a smile plastered on my face. But inside, my soul didn't match my outward expressions. I felt drained, as if energy were being sucked out of me with every conversation.

The next morning, the day of the wedding, I woke up feeling completely normal. We had breakfast with some of my aunts, uncles, and cousins at a restaurant called the Sundancer Grill. After checking out of our rooms around 10:30 AM, we headed to the Camp Lucy resort in Dripping Springs to check into the cabin.

The resort was gorgeous—a tranquil setting for a wedding weekend. We spent a few hours wandering the property, taking in the sights, chatting with old friends and relatives, and meeting new people.

If you can imagine the scene that unfolds in the hours leading up to every wedding throughout history, there are two distinct groups of people:

The group that takes four to five hours to attend to every hair on their head, dab each facial pore with the perfect amount of makeup, and, Lord knows, whatever else goes on throughout the afternoon.

Then there's the other group, also known as men.

So, while our wives spent the afternoon preparing themselves, the guys hung out on patios scattered throughout the property, pre-gaming and saving the last 45 seconds to throw on a suit and a pair of shoes.

The walk to the chapel was an easy two-minute stroll. Ian's Chapel wasn't your average wedding venue; it had a unique charm that blended history from different places and times. From the Events Hall to the open-air Pavilion to the Great Lawn, you could practically feel history seeping from every oak beam and timber. At the heart of it all was a restored French colonial chapel, built in the 1800s. The weathered stone walls could tell a thousand stories of couples saying, "I do."

The cocktail reception was set to be held right outside the chapel in an area known as "The Great Lawn," a beautiful grassy space with sweeping views of the countryside.

Ian's Chapel wasn't just a place to get married; it was a collection of cool, historic buildings ready to create the perfect wedding day atmosphere.

None of that mattered to me that day. By 4:15 PM, friends and family were taking their seats inside the chapel while cracks were already forming in my own personal foundation.

By the time the music started, it would be a full-on meltdown.

CHAPTER 20
THE PRESSURE CHAMBER

Ezekiel 37:5 *"This is what the Sovereign Lord says: Look! I am going to put breath into you and make you live again."*

There's a scene from *Fight Club*, my all-time favorite movie, where the narrator has a startling revelation. As he pieces together the shocking truth—that he and Tyler Durden are actually one and the same—his world unravels in an instant, like a sudden loss of cabin pressure. The realization hits all at once, disorienting him, suffocating him, until he finally collapses onto the hotel bed.[1]

Fortunately, the Navy trains us for this exact scenario (the cabin pressure part, not the split personality), because loss of cabin pressure at higher altitudes leads to hypoxia, which can be fatal. If you're not familiar with hypoxia, it's a condition where a lack of oxygen prevents your brain and body tissues from functioning properly.

And in layman's terms, that's bad. I didn't go to doctor school, but I remember from high school science class that your brain needs oxygen for thinking and stuff.

Every four years, aircrew undergo hypoxia training. This training coincides with water survival requalification, where participants demonstrate swimming and floating skills during a series of tests, including a simulated parachute entry over water, "drownproofing," and escaping from a downed helicopter in both daytime and nighttime conditions. The water survival part isn't really relevant to the story, but it's important to note that most aviators dread it. But the chamber ride during hypoxia training is awesome.

During hypoxia training, aircrew members enter a closed hypobaric chamber capable of replicating altitudes exceeding 20,000 feet. Participants range from newcomers to seasoned aviators taking the test for the fifth or sixth time in their careers. Instructors, wearing oxygen masks, serve as safety observers.

The "flight" begins at sea level, and aircrew members "ascend" to altitude. At 10,000 feet, most people begin to feel the effects of altitude—breathing becomes thinner, and the body may require 25 to 30% more energy to perform the same tasks as at sea level. We would be given simple tasks to perform, such as signing our names on a blank piece of paper, completing basic second-grade addition exercises like 12 + 7, or even playing patty cake with the person next to us.

Hypoxia sneaks up on you, but there are subtle clues, including decreased vision, confusion, or tingling and warm sensations throughout your body. The goal of the training is to help you understand the symptoms in your body, as everyone experiences them differently.

In the chamber, oxygen is your lifeline. Once you identify your symptoms, you simply reach down, grab the mask, put it on your face, flip the switch to start the flow of oxygen, and enjoy the rest of the ride while watching others struggle to add single-digit numbers together.

The same jokes and challenges surfaced every time I entered that chamber. "How long can you go before you pass out?" "Bet you'll be the last to put my mask on." There's always one guy who tries to tough it out. You'd notice his blue lips and laugh as he continued playing patty cake with himself, thinking that he was crushing it. One year, I thought I had a perfect score on my math paper, only to find out afterward that I wasn't even writing numbers at the end.

But don't worry—the instructors are always there to ensure everyone safely gets on oxygen.

The entire test is quite simple: know the signs, understand the available tools, treat yourself, and live.

When I was struggling, it wasn't that I didn't recognize the signs—I just thought they didn't apply to me. I believed I could suck it up and be tougher than the guy next to me. *Let that dummy over there struggle to add 12 + 7 together, which the answer is clearly 241 purple zebras. And why are my lips numb?*

And, if I knew what the signs were, surely I knew what kind of help was out there. In the chamber, the oxygen was right there when I needed it. I just had to reach out, put the mask on, and breathe it in. When I was struggling, I had friends I could call. A provider I could reach out to. My own wife would surely listen. There's even 988, the number I could call or text if it got really bad, but I was nowhere near that. And, if their comes a time when it acsully does get badd enuff, adn i cnt'e breeeeethed, 1'Ll juste go................."

Unconscious.

Until God decides to put breath back into me and make me live again.

CHAPTER 21
THE WEDDING, PART II

Psalm 31:9 *"Have mercy on me, Lord, for I am in distress. Tears blur my eyes. My body and soul are withering away."*

Saturday, December 31, 2022. 4:45 PM

T he ceremony was underway, and my brother stood at the front of the chapel, eagerly awaiting his beautiful bride's entrance. Friends and family had gathered from across the country to celebrate this glorious occasion, while simultaneously ringing in the New Year.

Though everything appeared fine on the surface, I felt a strange heaviness building inside me. I didn't know what it was, but I figured I could push through, just as I always had. The elephant had busted out of the box and was back, but this time it wasn't content to merely sit on my chest; it had brought some friends along.

I sat in a chair in the second row, staring off into nothingness, as though someone were dragging me down into an endless abyss of paranoia, sadness, and despair all at once. My brother's best friend and business partner was the officiant, and as he stood next to my brother at the front of the chapel, waiting for the bride to make her way down the aisle, I found myself in a distant place, lost in that abyss.

The voices at the front of the church became incoherent muttering—distant and garbled, like someone trying to talk to you while you're chained at the bottom of a pool, the weight of the water pressing in from all sides.

It felt as though someone had just cranked the thermostat up to 145 degrees.

I struggled to breathe as the weight of the world pressed down on my chest.

My knee bounced a million miles an hour.

I was sweating through my suit while simultaneously experiencing Arctic chills.

I needed to get out of there, but standing up in the middle of the wedding wasn't an option. I closed my eyes and hoped it would pass quickly.

"*Suck it up, buttercup,*" echoed in my head, over and over.

I avoided eye contact with anyone, which was easy since nobody was there to see me anyway. This wasn't my wedding; all eyes were on the bride and groom at the front of the chapel.

All I could think about was not being there. If I weren't there—whether deployed overseas or dead—nobody would miss me. They wouldn't even think twice about it. I know that's a lie, but I couldn't stop believing it, which only made me spiral further.

Eleanor, noticing something was off with me, whispered, "Are you okay?"

I nodded my head. She pulled a small white pill from her purse and gently placed it in my hand, then produced a bottle of water seemingly out of nowhere. She didn't know this was not the first Xanax I had taken that day, but I gladly swallowed it down to help me get through the rest of the service.

As the ceremony wrapped up, guests made their way to the lawn for post-wedding pictures. Music filled the air, guests struck up lively conversations, the cocktail line stretched throughout the pavilion, and hors d'oeuvres were passed around on silver trays.

I stood in a large circle of family members, trying to shake off what I'd just experienced while nursing a glass of tonic and lime, desperately attempting to fit in with those holding their cocktails. I couldn't bear to hear someone ask, "What, not drinking anything? You sick? You a chick or something?"

The wedding photos felt endless. I kept being called over for yet another group shot, and I might have even smiled once or twice for my Mom's sake. I just wanted to go home.

CHAPTER 22
UNSEEN BATTLES

Galatians 6:2 "*Share each other's burdens, and in this way obey the law of Christ.*"

I've known more than a handful of acquaintances, both military and civilian, who have tragically died by suicide. Among them were two very close friends: Kenny, whom I first met in Lemoore in 2005, and Joe, another E-2 NFO with whom I developed a close relationship over the years, both personally and professionally.

Mental health is a complex issue. I'm no expert, but I can share my own experiences and insights. Over the past few years, I've come to view three things differently:

1. **Recognizing the signs of someone struggling can be more challenging than you think.**

When news breaks about someone who has died by suicide, we often hear the same reactions:

- *"He had so much going for him, why would he do that?"*
- *"I had no idea he was struggling, everything seemed fine."*
- *"I knew he had problems, but I didn't realize it was that serious."*

Sound familiar? Trust me, I've repeated these sentences countless times.

In 2016, during my Skipper tour in California, I addressed my squadron during our annual suicide prevention training. While the Navy's standard set of slides was effective, I felt compelled to add a personal touch to connect on a more human level.

Standing at the front of the auditorium, I presented a few additional slides I had prepared earlier that week, hoping to resonate with the room in a way that felt real and personal.

The first slide was a screenshot of a text exchange between me and Kenny in the months leading up to his death. In this exchange, I had made a sarcastic comment about a Facebook post he shared, to which he replied, "…but I'm a shit show lately," accompanied by a sad face emoji.

I continued to poke fun at his use of emojis, and what followed were incoherent blurbs that ended with him calling himself an idiot.

Flying in Portugal with Kenny

At the time, lacking any other context, I chalked it up to drunken ramblings. It wouldn't have been the first time we talked nonsense over beers. Our families had become very close over the years, and even though we lived miles apart at that time, we still managed to see each other at least once a year.

With the benefit of hindsight, I could have picked up the phone and asked him about his life. Not the usual American question, "How's it going?" but rather sincerely ask how he was doing. Maybe I could have been the one to prevent his death, but I'll never know.

The second slide I showed featured a series of Facebook posts from Joe. He was someone I had gotten to know well during my Navy career, and the summer before his death, we spent a lot of time together in Florida and Virginia while undergoing flight refresher training. Whether we were playing golf or having drinks, the conversation was always light and easy.

In late September 2014, Joe first posted a picture of a stray dog he found running down the road near his apartment, asking the social media world if anyone knew the owner of this one-eyed creature missing several teeth. Over the following weeks, his posts continued on Facebook as he named the dog and began to care for him while still searching for the owner. On October 13, 2014, the dog suddenly passed away from cardiac arrest during a trip to the animal emergency room. Joe wrote a post expressing his frustration, saying, "Although I knew this guy for a short amount of time, this sucks."

About a week later, Joe died by suicide. I remember discussing this with a couple of mutual friends in the days following his death:

- He had so much going for him. Why would he do that?
- I mean, I had no idea he was struggling. We hung out just a few weeks ago, and it seemed like everything was going great.
- Well… I guess I knew he was dealing with a couple of small issues, but I didn't realize it was that serious.

I can't say for certain that his posts on Facebook had any significant meaning. But as I replayed them in my mind in the months after his passing, I felt a deep sense of guilt for not recognizing the signs that he was struggling.

As I looked out at the faces in the auditorium crowd, I tried to drive the point home: the signs are there, but they're not always what you

might expect. Sometimes, we just need to ask the simple question: "...
is everything okay with you?"

2. Getting help for mental health is not just for the "weak-minded."

A good friend of mine, another Navy captain, recently shared a story
from when he was the commanding officer at one of the larger U.S.
Navy bases. After one of the men who worked for him died by suicide,
my friend stood before the base auditorium and addressed the entire
command. He said all the right words and encouraged everyone to
seek help, telling them to take the time they needed to process the
tragedy.

Afterward, one of the counselors pulled him aside and asked, "How
are you doing?"

His reaction was automatic: "I'm good. This sucks, but I'm good."

She repeated the same question, this time with a softer tone, "No, how
are you doing for real?"

He responded a bit more firmly, "Seriously, I'm fine."

As my friend recounted this story, he admitted he was becoming frustrated by her persistence. He felt insulted, as though seeking help
somehow made him weak.

I've stood before my sailors and given the same speech: "It's okay to
ask for help." But when it came to my own struggles, I didn't believe
that applied to me. I thought asking for help meant I wasn't strong
enough.

3. When you're struggling, reaching out can be harder than one might think.

Over the past year, as I began to open up to a few close friends about
my experiences, I heard various well-intentioned statements like,

"Dude, I had no idea. You should have called me, man."

From my own experience, I can tell you I didn't want to talk to anyone. The very mentality that brought me to that point—that "suck it up" mindset—was the same thing that prevented me from reaching out for help. I viewed mental health as something one should be able to control. If you couldn't control it, then you were simply weak. I couldn't appear weak. I couldn't lose face in front of friends, family, coworkers, and especially not those I was leading.

Even when my wife tried to get me to talk, I couldn't. I didn't know what was wrong, and my pride prevented me from admitting that I couldn't control everything. That's when the thoughts in my head spiraled. I was consumed with ways to make the sadness go away—ways to lift the elephant off my chest. I searched for a box big enough to stuff my issues into, to hide them away in a closet where I wouldn't have to see them. I threw myself into work—anything but discussing what was going on.

So picking up the phone and texting a friend felt like a non-starter.

I thought I had everything under control, managing life's challenges with the same discipline I'd relied on for years. But sometimes, no matter how strong you think you are, the weight catches up with you.

That realization hit me hard in a way I never anticipated—right in the middle of my brother's wedding.

CHAPTER 23
THE WEDDING, PART III

Psalm 31:10 *"I am dying from grief; my years are shortened by sadness. Sin has drained my strength; I am wasting away from within."*

Saturday, December 31, 2022. 8:00 PM

Cocktail hour had ended, the outdoor photos were done, and it was time for guests to move into the Great Hall for the reception to begin. I shuffled in and took a seat next to my wife at one of the long tables, sitting across from the rest of my family. Everybody around me seemed to be screaming their heads off, though I couldn't focus on any of the words. Staring at my plate didn't help, it only intensified the noise in my head.

As the bride and groom entered, my head swam with anxiety, the sensation like treading water just to stay afloat. The conversation around me dissolved into distant muffled murmurs, blending with the ever-louder whispers of negativity clawing at my mind.

"You're worthless. You don't even belong here," I thought, as my mom stood to join my brother for the traditional mother-son dance.

Why are you such a pu$$y? Get your shit together.

Someone at the table cracked a joke about my brother's dance moves, the sound of laughter slicing through the haze in my head.

Everyone else here is having fun. Why are you such a miserable f*k?

Sweat beaded on my skin again, and it felt like the elephant had turned into a boa constrictor, slowly squeezing the air from my lungs.

I leaned over to Eleanor and whispered, "I gotta get out of here." I didn't wait to see if she heard me.

I stood up, turned right, and walked straight out into the cool desert evening. With no destination in mind and nowhere to escape the relentless noise in my head, I just kept walking. Tears burned behind my eyes, threatening to spill, while my hand instinctively gripped my chest, desperate to ease the crushing weight that made it impossible to breathe. The maroon tie I was wearing felt alive, constricting around my neck as if were actively trying to choke me.

My heart pounded violently against my ribcage.

Eleanor caught up with me as I rounded the front of Ian's Chapel.

"What's going on? Are you okay?" she asked, her concern sharp and urgent. "Ben... BEN!"

"I just need some air," I managed to say.

"But what's wrong?" she pressed, unwilling to let it go.

"I DON'T KNOW... I don't know. But I can't go back in there."

I collapsed on a bench and let my head fall into my hands. The tears had started to fall. "Please don't make me go back. PLEASE…"

After a few minutes, I stood up and wordlessly started to head back to our room. The walk from the chapel to our cabin was only three minutes, but it felt like three days. Once inside, I crawled onto the bed, still in my suit, and pulled the heavy comforter over my head, desperate to shut out the sorrow and the noise. My body was fully immersed in a game of fight-or-flight, and my nervous system had chosen flight. I could feel myself beginning to shut down.

Eleanor climbed into bed and gently wrapped her arms around me, though the embrace felt distant—like a gesture meant for someone else. "Are you okay?" she asked softly. "Can I get you anything?"

I probably would have asked the same questions in her shoes. I would have been just as confused as she was. This came out of nowhere, and it had nothing to do with the wedding or anyone there.

She lay beside me all night, her hand gently resting on my back, deflecting the texts and calls from people wondering where we were.

I was completely broken with no idea why. And I had no clue how to fix it.

I didn't want to talk to anyone. I didn't want to see anyone. I just wanted the pain to stop. I just wanted to close my eyes.

And if they never opened again, I would have been okay with that.

CHAPTER 24
THE CLOSET IS FULL

1 Peter 5:8 *"Stay alert! Watch out for your great enemy, the devil. He prowls around like a roaring lion, looking for someone to devour."*

Sunday, January 1, 2023. 7:15 AM

On Sunday morning, Eleanor drove all five of us home. Shortly after 7 AM, I shuffled to the minivan and slumped into the front seat, completely out of it. Only later did I realize that Eleanor had packed everything, woken the kids, and made sure we were ready to leave. I didn't care—I was just a shell of myself, a pile of flesh and bones, moving from point A to point B.

We skipped the post-wedding breakfast at my brother's house and left without saying goodbye. I couldn't face anyone that morning.

Eleanor told me later that I had stared out the window for most of the drive, completely silent. I kept mumbling to myself internally, *"…stop it…stop it….stop being weak."* But no matter how much I tried, those words were lost in the storm of chaos swirling through my mind.

After the meltdown at my brother's wedding, the days that followed were some of the darkest I've ever known. Suicidal thoughts consumed my mind, and every moment felt like a struggle just to keep my head above water. It was as though I were drowning in sorrow, submerged deep in an ocean of relentless negativity. There was no lifeline, no raft to climb into—just the crushing weight of it all, pulling me further into the darkness.

Fighting it was physically and mentally exhausting. I didn't have a specific plan yet, but I was reaching the point where I'd consider anything—*anything*—just to silence the storm raging in my head.

Monday seemed to begin on a better note—or so I thought. We ran some errands, giving our 15-year-old with a learner's permit a chance to get some driving practice.

I sat in the front seat, already anxious and on edge, watching his every move like a hawk.

When he failed to yield properly at a busy intersection, I absolutely lost it, yelling at him as if he were deliberately trying to kill us all.

Later, while we were shopping at an Old Navy, that dark cloud engulfed me once more. One moment I felt fine, and the next, I was suffocating under the burden of it all.

I had thought that the wedding weekend was just an anomaly, a glitch in my otherwise healthy system, but I was mistaken. The emotions kept crashing down on me at random, unexpected times, and I didn't know how to escape from beneath them.

I needed to get outside, away from the crowds, the bubblegum pop music that blared throughout the store, and the endless piles of cloth-ing. I didn't tell anyone; I simply left.

At some point, Eleanor spotted me across the parking lot, wandering aimlessly. She ushered the kids into the minivan, drove over to where I was walking, and silently rolled down the window as she came to a stop.

Without saying a word, I opened the passenger door and settled into my seat, my head pressed against the window for the entire drive home.

That afternoon, before I lay down, I asked Eleanor to change the combination to the gun safe. Some bad, bad plans were starting to formulate in my head, and I was terrified that I might slip into a state from which I couldn't recover.

She was clearly more worried than she had been yesterday, and seeing the tears in her eyes only deepened my distress. I had bailed on a wedding because I couldn't get a grip on my own emotions, and now I was dragging her and the kids down with me. I felt like I was becoming a burden to my family.

I didn't think my kids understood what was happening, and I was determined to keep it that way. I didn't want them to see their father falling apart.

Later that afternoon, I left the house without saying a word to anyone and drove to the Emergency Room. I thought that being physically there in the ER parking lot meant one of two things would happen: I would continue on this current nosedive while sitting just 200 feet from help, or I would find a way to suck it up, act like a man, and return to a life of normalcy.

I pulled into the half-full parking lot and sat in my truck, about five rows back from the entrance. I turned to my phone and began watching episodes of *It's Always Sunny in Philadelphia*, arguably one of the best shows ever created. Maybe I just needed a laugh to lift me out of this funk. My phone buzzed nonstop with Eleanor's texts and calls, but I wasn't in any state to talk to anyone—not even her. I needed to try to work through it on my own.

After that wave of sadness finally subsided, I drove back home, doing my best to slip through the door without anyone noticing. I felt embarrassed, and the shame hit me hard. I didn't want to see or talk to anyone; I just wanted to disappear.

A few minutes later, Eleanor found me in the bedroom closet, curled up on the floor with both of our dogs, the only company I could tolerate at that moment.

I still had cardboard boxes scattered throughout the walk-in closet, a reminder that I hadn't unpacked everything from our chaotic move to Texas back in August. I kept telling myself I'd get to them eventually, and that nobody had to see the mess in my closet but me anyway.

But the real mess wasn't there in the physical world. It was every little piece of unseen emotional baggage I'd compartmentalized, crammed into boxes, and shoved deep into the recesses of my mind. I no longer had the ability to suck it up; there was no more room in the closet. And now, like some kind of explosion, those hidden feelings had spilled out and scattered everywhere, suffocating me with years of unresolved pain.

I was sobbing uncontrollably, having completely lost control, my body shaking as if I'd just run out of fuel. Eleanor quietly slipped into the closet and found me lying in the dark. She didn't say anything at first; she simply placed a hand on my shoulder.

I couldn't look up. There was this strange mix of comfort in her presence, but at the same time, I felt awful for her witnessing me like this— falling apart, crumbling under the weight of all the things I'd been avoiding.

She sat on the floor next to me, and in that quiet way she has, said, "I'm here, it's OK." No questions. No pushing—just letting me know I wasn't alone. The dogs scooted a little closer, as if they could sense what was happening. I felt as vulnerable as I had ever been, lying there in the dark. But strangely, there was also this tiny bit of relief in finally letting it all out.

A few minutes later, she left and then returned with her phone in hand.

"Hey," she said, her voice barely above a whisper. "I have someone on the phone that I know. He said he can help you. Want to talk to him for a few minutes?"

I didn't want to. But as she sat there next to me, silently, phone in hand, tears streaming down her face, I knew that I had to.

"Yeah," I said into the phone, trying to sound as if I hadn't been sobbing just 30 seconds ago.

"Hi, Ben. My name is Jason, and your wife tells me that you're going through some things. Can we talk for a few minutes?"

God, not this again. I didn't want to take walks or a bubble bath. I didn't want pills; I just wanted it all to stop.

But Jason and I ended up talking for about 30 minutes, and by the end, I agreed to meet with him in a few days.

CHAPTER 25
TOO MANY PEAS ON MY PLATE

Proverbs 20:5 *"The purposes of a person's heart are deep waters, but one who has insight draws them out."*

Wednesday, January 4, 2023. 4:00 PM

Jason was a counselor Eleanor had recently been introduced to through a friend. With his military and first responder background, he seemed like the perfect person to understand what I was going through.

Our first session was four days after my brother's wedding, and I was feeling pretty down. But as I logged into Zoom that Wednesday for our first session, I did my best to put on a brave face. After all, that's what I'd always been trained to do, and it was clear I'd be talking to another Alpha male. What was I supposed to do—lie on the couch and cry while he hypnotized me? That's what I thought effective counseling looked like, especially since my last few attempts had been miserable experiences.

Thankfully, unlike my previous experiences with counselors, we didn't waste the first session going over every detail I had already shared in the consultation forms.

"So, I know we talked the other day, but why don't you tell me a little more about what's been happening?" Jason started.

"Well," I began. "I'm not exactly sure what's going on. I've been having these feelings of anxiety and thoughts of dying, but I have no idea where they're coming from. I've been 'successful' in my career, I have a great family, and it's not like I've experienced any major tragedy in my life."

Jason nodded as he jotted down notes, keeping eye contact with me while I spoke.

"I didn't witness a bus full of nuns die in a crash, and my parents didn't beat me or chain me up in the basement," I continued, using humor to deflect and downplay the reality of what had been happening.

What Jason said next brought so much clarity that I broke down in tears right there on the spot.

"Most guys like you are in the same boat, especially with a background in the military or as first responders," Jason explained. "Think of it like this: if every stressor in your life were a tiny pea on a plate, dealing with just one wouldn't be a big deal. After all, it's only a pea. But if you ignore those peas, if you don't address what's on your plate, they start to pile up. Eventually—and usually when you least expect it—the plate gets so full that it topples over. Sometimes it happens at the worst possible moment, like at your brother's wedding. Our goal now is to start eating those peas one by one, so your plate becomes manageable."

That visualization has been brilliant for me over the past year. It provided a mental framework for handling life's stresses instead of boxing them up and ignoring them. Or, in Jason's words, letting them pile up on the plate unacknowledged. Over the course of a few weeks, Jason helped me recognize things I had never dealt with in a healthy way.

I began talking about Pappy's funeral. I cried for five minutes, realizing I had never properly grieved when he passed away in January

2020. Then, I talked about Kenny and Joe—losses I had experienced but ignored, choosing to press on. I also talked about Chud, my cruise roommate and best friend, and how he was diagnosed with terminal cancer in 2020 and passed away a few short months later.

I spoke with Chud twice before he passed—first on a group video call with mutual friends shortly after he broke the news to me, and a few weeks later, over the phone. We traded text messages every now and then, but I knew he was probably getting bombarded and tried to give him some space.

In October 2020, we were driving from DC to North Carolina for a family vacation. Since we were passing by Norfolk, VA, I thought we might stop in to see him, but when he texted me back, he said it wasn't a good idea. I knew then that he was too weak for visitors.

When the news came that he had passed right before Thanksgiving, I was on my way to Austin to visit family and didn't attend the funeral. At the time, I wasn't even sure if visitors would be allowed due to the ever-changing COVID regulations, and I would have missed Thanksgiving because of the travel.

One of my biggest life regrets is choosing to continue on to Austin instead of attending his funeral.

As Jason helped me process my grief, I would often hang up after our sessions and sit at my desk, crying with my head in my hands, wishing I had let this out years earlier instead of trying to suppress it. Eventually, I'd pull myself together, wipe my face, and log back into my work computer, forcing myself to set it all aside and focus.

Over the next few weeks, I noticed my mental state starting to improve, but I knew there was still a long road ahead. It's no surprise —unpacking 40+ years of suppressed emotions isn't something that happens overnight. Have you ever tried to quit a deeply ingrained habit cold turkey or change a behavior that's been part of you for decades? It's exhausting, and it requires relentless effort.

Yet, I continued to seesaw between the highs and lows. Some days, I felt completely normal. I showed up at work with a smile, attended my kids' sporting events, chatted with other parents, and engaged in life. On other days, I'd wake up wishing I could go back to sleep and never open my eyes again. I still lacked the mental courage or strength to learn the new code for the gun safe.

One Saturday, after a few sessions with Jason, Eleanor and I stopped for lunch after doing some typical weekend shopping. While we were sitting at our table talking, a wave of sadness suddenly crashed over me, literally mid-sentence. My mind began to shut down, and tunnel vision set in. I felt as though I was reaching for an oxygen mask but couldn't find it. I waited for a natural break in the conversation, and when our salads arrived, I stood up to go to the bathroom. I stood in front of the mirror and splashed water on my face, not even able to recognize the person staring back at me. Right then, I decided I couldn't stay any longer, so I exited the restaurant without returning to the table.

That's right. I stepped out of the men's bathroom, walked behind the table where my wife was waiting for me to return, and then exited through the doors into the parking lot without saying a word. Yes, it's completely irrational, but my mind was telling me I needed to be home in the safety of my bed, and the only way to get there was to start walking.

The problem was that our house was 13 miles away. And Eleanor didn't even know I left.

I think I made it about half a mile before sitting down on a curb in the corner of a shopping center parking lot. I was exhausted, and I couldn't see through the tears in my eyes. I ignored her text messages and phone calls, which were increasing in frequency and urgency. Honestly, I don't know what was going through my head, but I'm very grateful for the invention of apps that show your location. Eventually, she drove over to where I was and picked me up, bringing me back home safely. I could tell she was mad. Like REALLY mad, and I didn't even know how to apologize. We spent the rest of the day in complete silence.

I was filled with shame and I wanted to bury that event. What was I going to say to my therapist? "Hey Jason, I ditched my wife in a restaurant and tried to take a five-hour walk home the other day. That's pretty normal, right?"

I was making decent progress but had a lapse, yet I continued to fight through the emotional lows with Jason's help.

After meeting with him for a couple of months, I felt like I had hit a plateau.

Maybe this is as good as it gets.

I still found myself psyching up before going to work or participating in social events, all while shoving my emotions back into the box and sticking it on the shelf. I was digesting a couple of the peas, but for the most part, I was just flicking them off the plate one at a time. I still didn't want to deal with everything all at once. It was too much, especially since I could just put on a happy face and pretend I was better.

Despite all that, counseling served its purpose by allowing me to be vulnerable and open up slightly. It was the start of my healing, and I was starting to move the elephant. Most of the time, I was actually feeling better about myself.

But there was so much more to come, and so much more work to be done.

CHAPTER 26
BUYING A NEW HOUSE

Matthew 7:24-25 *"Anyone who listens to my teaching and follows it is wise, like a person who builds a house on solid rock. Though the rain comes in torrents and the floodwaters rise and the winds beat against that house, it won't collapse because it is built on bedrock."*

Tuesday, March 14, 2023. 7:15 PM

On a perfect spring evening in northern Texas, Eleanor and I were at a local park watching Nora play lacrosse. As the game unfolded, our conversation shifted to the house that we had been renting since moving to Texas. The lease was expiring in four months, and it felt like the right time to start looking for our forever home. First, we needed to find a realtor.

"Well, Cindy was amazing when we moved here," Eleanor said. "Why don't I text her to see if she's up for coffee or a drink next week? It'd be good to meet her in person, and we can talk strategy."

Eleanor sent a text, and Cindy replied within minutes with a better idea. "There's a house that just came on the market and it's in a fantastic neighborhood. I think you guys will love it. Why don't we meet over there around 6:00 tomorrow night? I'll send you the details in the morning."

The next day, I was staring at a seller disclosure statement and the listing details when something caught my eye. I was working from home and walked downstairs to find Eleanor in her office. "Did you see that email?" I asked. "What does it mean that there's a 'crack in the foundation'? No thanks. Not interested."

Thanks to my in-depth knowledge of house structure and real estate, gained exclusively through HGTV property flipping shows, I wasn't about to get caught up in a money pit.

Then I learned about foundations in Texas. Apparently, most fall into these categories: A) those with cracks that haven't been fixed yet, B) those with cracks that have been repaired, or C) those just waiting to crack. As we stood in the driveway discussing it, Cindy reassured us about the repairs that had already been completed and the warranty that was transferable.

From the moment we stepped into the house, Eleanor and I knew it was the one. In fact, I think we knew it before we even passed through the front door. We toured the bedrooms, bathrooms, the main areas, and the backyard with its little fishpond, all in about 10 minutes. There was just something about the place that spoke to us. So when Cindy asked, "What do y'all think?"

"We love it," we both said, almost simultaneously.

She took us to one more property a few blocks away, but before we even walked through the door, we knew it was a waste of time. We lasted about 90 seconds in the house, didn't even bother going upstairs, and then regrouped outside.

"So, why don't y'all take the night to talk it over, and let me know what you're thinking tomorrow?" Cindy said.

I took one look at Eleanor, and she confirmed what I was thinking without saying a word. "Actually, we want to put an offer on the house," I said.

Cindy looked at me, then looked at Eleanor, and raising an eyebrow asked, "Are you sure? Just like that?"

"Yep, we're sure. We've been through this enough times to know what we want, and that house is it."

Both of us could sense the excitement and anticipation of putting down roots and growing our futures together here, and we knew it instantly.

Despite knowing the foundation had cracks, we still loved everything about the house. After all, nothing is perfect.

But, the universe has a way of testing your foundations when you least expect it.

About two weeks later, my entire team at work received strange 15-minute meetings added to our Friday calendars. One by one, we were all laid off by the new manager, a person I'd only had a single 30-minute conversation with. It was a crushing blow—one that came completely out of nowhere. We left all our friends and moved from Virginia to Texas nine months ago to start a new phase. We worked through all the stressful parts of transitioning from the Navy. My team was making great progress at work, and I was shedding the imposter suit that I wore my first few months on the job. We were just a few weeks away from closing on a new house. We had finally made it.

And now I didn't have a job.

I had to start the post-military job search all over again, in a city where I didn't really know anyone.

But there were bigger issues lurking—ones that didn't show up in any disclosure statement.

I just didn't know it yet.

CHAPTER 27
GINA DOES WHAT?

Ecclesiastes 11:5 "*As you do not know what is the way of the wind, or how the bones grow in the womb of her who is with child, so you do not know the works of God who makes everything.*"

Monday, August 28, 2023. 6:45 PM

For most of my life, I've been skeptical about many things. I've always struggled to believe in ideas I couldn't see, touch, or fully grasp. This skepticism spanned across various areas, from religious beliefs and the existence of God, to ghosts and spirits, aliens and mysterious "UFOs"—even the Boogeyman.

For years my wife would talk about how the Universe showed her signs. She'd always point out the number 42 whenever it popped up—whether on a license plate, the TV, or even a Chinese takeout menu. To her, seeing that number was the Universe's way of confirming whatever was on her mind. For me, the number 42 just means it's Jackie Robinson Day, or that I'm about to order Moo Shu Pork.[1]

Similarly, she was a firm believer in manifesting things—whether it was a successful business, a relationship, or even something material. For six months, I listened to her talk about manifesting a new SUV to replace our old, hail-damaged, kid-stained minivan.

Right… I'll just keep 'thinking' about that brand-new car, and it'll magically appear in our driveway. Oh, and while I'm at it, how about I manifest 10 pounds off my gut?

Considering my stubborn mindset up to this point, it's no surprise my wife never fully explained the hour-long blocks on her calendar over the past couple of years, when she was meeting with Gina.

Alright, let me clarify. Eleanor wasn't running around behind my back. She wasn't "seeing somebody on the side." She wasn't really hiding anything. In fact, she probably told me about Gina's work on multiple occasions, I just wasn't listening.

Gina is an energy healer who specializes in releasing trapped emotions.

By this point in my life, I was finally open to counseling. I could see the benefits and realized there were still mental puzzles I needed to work through. But trapped emotions? That sounded like complete nonsense. What's next—calling someone to banish the Boogeyman lurking under the bed, ready to sprinkle bad juju on you while you sleep? Just go for a run or knock out fifty push-ups and shake off your "emotions" while saving me some cash in the process.

It turns out my mind needed to be stretched a bit further. I knew my wife and Gina were meeting regularly, and at first, I thought Gina was just a counselor helping her with everyday issues. Every time my wife had a session with Gina, she came away feeling better. Who wouldn't want that for their spouse?

As I later discovered, Gina is a certified Emotion Code and Body Code practitioner, and a wonderful person I've grown to love and respect for how she helps others. The Emotion Code, developed by Dr. Bradley Nelson, is a holistic healing technique designed to release trapped emotions believed to cause physical and emotional issues.[2] Practitioners use techniques like muscle testing and specific methods to identify and release these trapped emotions, with the belief that doing so can alleviate various physical symptoms and emotional challenges.

That summer, as I continued to wrestle with my own emotions, we also grew increasingly concerned about one of our children, who was facing some teenage struggles. His "gloomy" behavior had persisted for about six years, dating back to our time in Southern California. This coincided with the onset of my health issues, though I never considered the possibility of a connection between the two. Eleanor and I spent many nights discussing options, thinking that connecting him with a therapist would be a good idea.

What I didn't know was that Eleanor had already connected Gina with our son, and they were actively working together to uncover any trapped emotions that might be impacting his emotional well-being.

On Monday, August 28th, my wife sat me down in the kitchen and played a recording from Gina that completely stopped me in my tracks.

That night, I scheduled a session with Gina to see if she could help me too.

CHAPTER 28
THE SHADOWS OF OUR HOME

Proverbs 3:33 *"The Lord's curse is on the house of the wicked, but he blesses the home of the righteous." (NIV)*

Monday, August 28, 2023. 7:15 PM

A few weeks after we moved into our new house in Texas—the one with the repaired foundation—Eleanor was invited to a neighborhood book club event just down the street. During the event, she learned from a neighbor that our house had a connection to a tragic and senseless crime involving a previous resident.

While the specifics of those events aren't relevant to this book, to tell my full story, I need to explain what led me to contact Gina. In the recording I heard, Gina, unaware of the house's history, described the dark, malevolent energy she sensed around the house.

And to answer the question that might be forming in your mind, there was no possible way Gina could have known anything about this house. None at all.

On August 28th, as Eleanor held up her phone and pressed play, I sat for ten minutes, listening as Gina uncovered things that were nearly impossible to comprehend.

Gina described a house haunted by a troubled past, with a dark energy that still lingered.

Stay with me for a moment, and press the "I Believe" button—because I had to. The terms and phrases she used sounded like something straight out of a horror movie.

She mentioned a dark energy score that was off the charts—more than 100%. And I didn't even know that was possible.

She identified 57 negative entities, each ranked 9 out of 10 in power, which, to me, sounded incredibly strong.

Shivers ran down my spine as she spoke of 12 curses so powerful they were "off the charts," including one specifically designed to prevent anyone entering the home from connecting with others.

Wait. What?

I had been searching for a new job, without success.

Our son was struggling in school and having a hard time making friends.

Eleanor's business was floundering—she had zero clients.

What is happening right now?

Gina continued, naming specific negative emotions tied to the house: physical trauma, helplessness, hopelessness, low self-esteem, and unworthiness.

She mentioned the overwhelming presence of red—like blood, tied to entities or memories of past events.

And then she talked about another 2,941 powerful, dark entities.

No big deal—just thousands of soul-sucking, evil things floating around my house.

She even identified a "saboteur energy" linked to the area where the driveway was built, dating back many years. The precision with which Gina described these elements was not only unsettling; it was terrifying. She was uncovering connections that challenged any conventional wisdom I had ever known.

Thankfully, she didn't just leave us hanging: "Hey, your house is cursed. Good luck!" As her message continued, she explained the steps she had taken to cleanse the house and promote healing. Though I didn't fully understand her methods and techniques, I trusted the process and hit my personal "I Believe" button. After listening to Gina's interpretation, it felt as though the house itself was speaking, sharing secrets of its troubled past.

If she could clear the house of negative energy, maybe she could help me, too.

I had to talk to her.

CHAPTER 29
GINA STARTS THE HEALING

Jeremiah 30:17 *"I will give you back your health and heal your wounds," says the Lord.*

Tuesday, August 29, 2023. 11:00 AM

L
ooking back on my sessions with Gina, I don't believe it's merely a coincidence that we found this exact house. I believe it was always God's plan for us to live here, so we could rewrite its story.

This house now represents a space for healing and the creation of new memories. It reminds us that, despite its past, we have the power to transform our surroundings and create positive experiences, even in the face of dark shadows from history.

But on the day that I had my first video session with Gina, I didn't know what to expect. And to my surprise, I felt nervous as we began.

She broke the ice by starting with a prayer: "I ask for a direct connection to God, to receive all answers through this channel, and that this healing be for Ben's highest truth and good."

Ok, that's an interesting start. God is involved here?

After the prayer, Gina said, "So, I know a little bit about you from Eleanor, but why don't you tell me a bit about what's going on?"

This question was familiar. *Oh, no. Is that how all these sessions start off?*

Despite my initial hesitancy, I knew in my heart that this was going to be different. "I didn't think I believed in any of this stuff," I said. "But after listening to your message last night, I'm willing to give this a shot." I opened up to her, sharing all my struggles from the past year. I told her how I lacked clarity about the next steps in my career, and how I wasn't sure about my identity anymore.

After getting everything off my chest, I felt a little better. Gina was taking notes, occasionally glancing at another screen as I spoke. Then she asked, "Do you have pain anywhere in your body?"

I laughed. "Yeah, you could say that."

I began listing the physical toll my body had endured over the years.

"My neck, right shoulder, lower back, right elbow, knee… to start."

Decades of wrestling, coaching, and countless hours in airplanes, along with enduring controlled "crashes" on aircraft carriers (also known as "arrested landings"), had left their mark. And, as every aviator knows, when you go in for your yearly physical, there is absolutely NOTHING wrong with you—or at least that's what you tell the flight surgeon. You put that pain in a box, stick it in the closet, limp out of the exam room, and get back to flying.

Suck it up, buttercup.

Gina began asking questions, occasionally glancing at her computer while maintaining a steady dialogue in her head. She explained the relationship between emotions and energy in simple terms. "Imagine walking into a party where everyone is having a great time," she began. "The energy in the room is positive, and even if you weren't feeling it when you walked in, you can't help but be lifted up. Now, imagine the opposite, and how negative energy can affect you. If you have a negative experience, you're more likely to feel negative emotions. And if you have an injury or illness, these emotions or energies can get trapped in your body, especially around areas of inflammation, infection, or injured tissues."

"Makes sense," I said.

Not really.

"So, your subconscious is aware of these emotions and energies," she continued. "I can test to see if any exist and then help to clear them." I later learned that this process is called applied kinesiology, or muscle testing.

Then, with pinpoint accuracy, she began identifying timeframes in my life when things seemed to go wrong.

"I'm seeing a lack of control that led to embarrassment, and this is from age six. Does that bring anything up for you?"

Umm... wait, so like when I peed my pants in kindergarten and everyone laughed at me?

"Yes," I said. I gave a short version of what happened.

"Great. I'm also picking up trapped emotions of despair and helplessness around your thyroid. This would have been when you were about 46 years old and could have manifested as pain. Does anything come to mind from that timeframe?"

Ummmm... like when I went to the doctor last year, complaining of difficulty swallowing and fearing that I'd developed throat cancer?

"Yes," I said, recapping that story too.

The session continued in this manner, with her identifying the trapped emotions, attempting to determine their source, and then working to clear them. During that first session, we focused on my lower back, where I've experienced pain for decades.

Those pains lingered long after I sat out that year of college wrestling. There were times when I struggled to stand upright after prolonged periods of sitting or lying down. Constant tension gripped my lower back, tightening with every movement and creating a persistent ache that was impossible to ignore. The discomfort often began as a dull, nagging pain but quickly escalated into sharp, stabbing sensations if I shifted my position or engaged in any physical activity.

The stiffness was especially pronounced in the morning, making it difficult to get out of bed and start my day. Even simple tasks, like bending over to tie my shoes or picking up a light object, became arduous challenges. The pain was not just a physical burden; it affected my mood and energy levels, often leaving me feeling frustrated and irritable.

It sounds like I should have seen a doctor, right? But that would mean admitting weakness.

As I listened to Gina call out various times in my life when emotions might have been trapped due to an injury, you could still call me skeptical. Each time, she recited words and phrases that sounded foreign to me—half prayer and half something else. Then she would check again to confirm that the negative emotions had been released.

"Okay, so the lack of control is at zero, and the feelings of helplessness and failure are gone too," Gina said after a ten-minute deep dive into my back. "I also identified an energy cord with your grandfather, linked by a shared compound of despair, failure, and helplessness."

"Oh, great," I said, trying to rally my belief behind the words. *So you just say some words and energy vanishes? Yep, that makes sense.*

I was focusing on that thought for a minute, and then her last sentence started to sink in. *And what's this stuff about my grandfather?*

In that moment, I wasn't convinced. On one hand, she was identifying things that nobody else could know. On the other hand, these generic questions and statements could apply to anyone. I couldn't help but think of the TV psychics who stand in front of a crowd and say, "I'm thinking of the name that starts with the letter 'C'… does anyone know a 'C' name who has died? You, sir, in the front row—do you know a 'C' name? What's that? Clifford? YES, that's it, Clifford. Clifford wants to tell you he says 'Hello.'"

Does this Emotion Code mumbo jumbo really work?

The next day, as I was waking up that Wednesday morning, I discovered the answer to that question.

Yes. Yes, it does.

My back was entirely free of pain and tension, and I felt like I was 18 again.

And there was more to come.

CHAPTER 30
MY PAPPY

Proverbs 17:6 *"Grandchildren are the crowning glory of the aged; parents are the pride of their children."*

My grandmother, Betty, passed away in July 1992, during the summer before my junior year of high school. Twenty-eight years later, in January 2020, my grandfather, Stu "Pappy" Albert, passed away—just before COVID changed the world. I took his death pretty hard, feeling as though there were so many things I hadn't said. I never told him that I loved him, just thinking that there would be more time. But I had the chance to make up for some of that when I was asked to deliver the eulogy at his funeral. In the days leading up to it, I gathered every letter he had written to me, every newspaper clipping he'd sent, every birthday card, and every memory I had of him.

Pappy had been in the hospital for a few days before his passing. The day before we packed up the car for Pennsylvania to attend the funeral, three envelopes arrived in the mail for my kids. When they opened them to find handwritten notes and gift cards, I broke down in tears. Even though he lay in a hospital bed, knowing his hours on this earth were numbered, his thoughts were still with others.

At his funeral, I stood before hundreds to deliver the eulogy, holding up his letters, newspaper clippings, and the three handwritten notes.

There were so many stories I could have shared, each one showing how selfless he was—always the first to help, never asking for anything in return. I mentioned our cross-country drive through St. Louis and his silent trip to the ER as an example of how he quietly carried his own struggles while always being there for others. The entire time, I felt his presence in the room. I could hear his words and laughter, as if he were sitting right beside me, watching. I could see the tears welling in his eyes and sense his humble pride, quietly honored that so many had gathered to say goodbye.

I thought I would never feel his presence again, but I was wrong. Gina had a message for me that changed everything.

CHAPTER 31
GINA SESSION 4

Deuteronomy 18:10-11 *"…And do not let your people practice fortune-telling, or use sorcery, or interpret omens, or engage in witchcraft, or cast spells, or function as mediums or psychics, or call forth the spirits of the dead."*

Wednesday, September 20, 2023. 2:00 PM

It was our fourth session together, and for the first time in my life, I looked forward to talking about everything that was happening to me. I was openly discussing my experiences without feeling judged or gaslit. Best of all, I was making progress, both mentally and physically.

Gina continued to identify trapped emotions linked to different physical ailments in my body. She connected the sadness in my neck to the loss of Joe in 2014, linked my right elbow issue to Kenny's death in 2015, and tied my shoulder pain to Chud's passing in 2020 after his brief battle with cancer.

On this particular day, we were discussing motivation and energy. I mentioned my struggle to get back into a workout routine. Previous counselors hadn't properly addressed this issue, and I felt stuck with a lack of motivation and persistent injuries that made lifting, running, or biking nearly impossible.

One of those persistent injuries was my right knee. It didn't bother me when I was at rest, but it flared up with activity, or even walking up or down steps. Just a few mornings earlier, I'd tried to go for a run, but I only lasted about two blocks before the pain forced me to stop and limp back home.

In the middle of her sentence, Gina abruptly paused, looking intently around as if someone were speaking to her. After a moment, her eyes returned to mine and she said, "I'm not sure if you're ready to hear this…" Her voice had slowed considerably, and her words were deliberate. It was like she had seen a ghost.

"Gina, we've talked about some crazy stuff, I don't think you could shock me with anything at this point."

Wrong.

"Okay…" she began. "I'm not a medium, but I'm hearing from your grandfather. Your grandmother is here too, but he's the one speaking. He's saying you need to leave the house."

"Huh?" I stared at her, dumbfounded. After what felt like thirty seconds, I managed to ask, "What do you mean my grandfather is there?"

Then the second part hit me. "Wait. We need to leave the house? We just moved in like two months ago!"

Gina continued, "They're showing me that there's something wrong with the house. There's something attached to it, and it's causing the problems you've been having. It's not something you have to deal with today, but at some point, you will need to leave."

Then she stopped, as if listening to an unseen presence off-screen. "I want to check on something," she said.

Oh, ok. I needed a moment to digest this. *Am I on one of those hidden camera shows? I can't be, that would take too mu —*

"I'm picking up something that happened when you were about twelve," Gina asked, interrupting my stream of thoughts. "Is there anything involving spirits from your childhood?"

Yes. Shit. Ouija board with Jake.

BACK IN TATAMY, IN THE 1980S...

When I was a kid living in Tatamy, we somehow came into possession of a Ouija board. You know, the game where everyone thinks someone else is moving the piece (called a "planchette") around to scare the others? I think we found it in my grandparents' attic among the vintage toys from the 1950s and '60s. Or maybe someone brought it over and left it. I can't really remember.

Either way, I was fascinated by the board. My friend Jake and I probably played with it the most. Jake lived a few streets away and came from a very religious family, so there was no chance that board would be allowed in his house. We played it a few times at my house, with moderate success. We'd ask silly questions, like "Does Amy like me?" and then wait forever as the piece moved at a snail's pace across the board to spell out "NO."

Jake and I had another friend who lived a few houses down, and the planchette moved at lightning speed whenever we took the board over to her house and asked the same questions. Some pretty wild stories circulated around town about supernatural events that occurred in that house. Multiple people reported seeing demonic apparitions in the fireplace. Strange noises were heard at night that were never explained. Supposedly, a family member was heavily into witchcraft. I'm sure the stories have been embellished over the years, but we believed every last one of them. And, it made for great gameplay with the board.

I remember one summer when Jake and I were about twelve years old, sitting cross-legged on the floor with a Ouija board between us. We were "talking" to a spirit—at least, that's what we told ourselves. In reality, we were just a couple of kids asking silly pre-teen questions, trying to make each other laugh.

One of us asked aloud, "What's your name?"

148

The planchette slowly crept across the board: J...O...H...N.

"John?" we asked in unison, struggling to keep a straight face.

The piece flew over to the word "YES."

"Are you dead?"

We busted up laughing, the absurdity of it all breaking our concentration. It took a few seconds to regain composure and put our "serious" faces back on, and the planchette spelling out "YES" helped.

"How old were you when you died?"

1.....2.....

"Twelve?"

"YES."

We fired off more questions in rapid succession: Where did you die? How did you die? Where are you now? The only answer that made any sense was "TREE." Naturally, we asked, "Did you fall out of a tree?"

"YES."

And just like that, we had our own special connection with John, the twelve-year-old spirit who supposedly fell out of a tree and died. Every time we brought out the board that summer, we asked for John, and he (or it?) always seemed to answer.

There were times when the planchette flew across the board so quickly, we could barely keep our fingers on it. By that point, Jake and I had long stopped accusing each other of moving it. Whether it was our combined imagination or something more, we never figured it out —but John became an oddly consistent part of our summer adventures.

One summer afternoon, curiosity got the better of me, and I asked John if he knew when we were going to die. It was a reckless question, especially for a couple of twelve-year-old boys messing around with a Hasbro board game. And before I could even get the last word out, the planchette started moving, Jake shot up, grabbed the board, and hurled it against the wall.

"NO WAY, DUDE!"

"Okay, okay, I was just kidding," I said, holding my hands up in surrender.

I wasn't.

I walked over, picked up the board, and brought it back to the coffee table. "I won't ask that again. Come on, let's play."

Reluctantly, Jake sat back down. I placed my fingers on the planchette and said, "I'm sorry, John."

Nothing.

"Are you there?"

Nothing. No movement at all. No matter what we asked or how many times I apologized, the planchette refused to budge.

Whatever. Stupid spirit.

We put the board away that day, and I think we might have pulled it out a few more times that summer only to lose interest as we started paying more attention to girls.

Looking back, I'm not sure what I believed at the time. On the surface, I enjoyed the thrill of having our own personal fortune teller—one who was our age and supposedly harmless. Even if we were talking to a "spirit," what could it really do? Throw the plastic planchette at me? Knock over my bookshelf in the middle of the night?

On some level, I understood that we were dabbling in something beyond a simple game, but I didn't care.

I should have.

BACK WITH GINA

I told Gina about my experience with the Ouija board. She nodded, confirming that I had nailed it.

Gina continued, "And then something similar when you were forty?"

"Yes," I replied, recalling our house in Camarillo. This was getting weirder.

CHAPTER 32
THE CALIFORNIA HOUSE

Psalm 91:11 *"For he will order his angels to protect you wherever you go."*

In 2014, when we moved from Germany to California, we were fortunate to find a beautiful home in Camarillo, just a 10-minute drive from the base. It was a newer house with a thoughtful, open layout: a staircase off the living room led directly to an upstairs landing, where three bedrooms, a children's bathroom, and a laundry room were arranged in a square. The boys shared a bunk bed in one room, while Nora's room—closest to the master bedroom—was directly across from the staircase.

Despite its modernity, strange things occasionally happened. At the time, we dismissed them as nonsense, or at best the quirks of a busy household. In the still of the night, toys from her bedroom would suddenly turn on, startling us out of a deep sleep. One toy in particular was a dollhouse with a small mailbox on the front. We would hear the doorbell ring, the dog bark, and all sorts of annoying sounds that no one wants to hear at 3:15 AM.

Yes, this happens to every parent in the world. It was probably the batteries or a faulty switch. Maybe the cat bumped the button and bolted as soon as the dollhouse sprang to life.

In the master bedroom, I had a touch lamp beside my bed, one of the first purchases I'd made with my very own adult money. It had three settings: dim, medium, and bright. It cast just the right amount of light for me to read at night, without shining too much on the other side of the bed where it might disturb my wife. About once a week, it would switch on by itself in the middle of the night, usually between 3 and 4 AM, always directly to the brightest setting.

I chalked it up to faulty wiring or accidental bumps and I became conditioned to simply reach over, tap it off, and go back to sleep. But after about a year of these unsolicited early-morning wake-ups, the lamp finally went into the trash.

During the three years we lived in that house, I spent a lot of time away, leaving Eleanor to manage the household and care for our children while I was deployed or on training missions. After one extended absence, we sat outside one evening, talking while the kids were in bed. That's when she told me about something strange that had happened while I was gone.

"I'm in bed, it's the middle of the night, and something wakes me up," she began. "I open my eyes, still lying there, and there's just enough light from the moon and the nightlights for me to see into the hallway. I see a fuzzy, translucent figure—like a woman in a flowy white dress or a sheet. It's floating right between the bathroom and laundry room, watching the entire top floor from that exact spot. The strangest part is, I'm not scared or startled at all. I just acknowledge it's there and go back to sleep."

"Does it say or do anything?" I asked, stifling what I thought were some pretty witty comments. *"Can she do laundry while she's just standing there?"*

"No," she replied. "It just floats there, watching."

"And it's *not* a dream?" I asked, clearly trying to poke holes in her story.

"Nope. Definitely not," she answered.

Somebody isn't getting enough sleep.

"Maybe you should close the door so it doesn't disturb you," I suggested, trying not to laugh.

Eleanor replied, "I have to leave it open, otherwise I won't hear the kids."

I wrote that experience off as just an overactive imagination. Maybe I "gaslit" her a little too much.

But then a few weeks after Christmas, while putting away decorations, I saw something that chilled me to the bone. Beneath the staircase was a small storage closet, just big enough to hold about eight Rubbermaid bins. We had just finished taking down the lights, stockings, and all the typical Christmas décor, shoving them back into bins that would remain in darkness until the following November. After stacking all the bins inside the storage space, I turned off the light and closed the door.

"Wait," Eleanor said, "there's one more we forgot."

I reopened the door and lugged the last bin inside without turning on the light. Since it was dark and my body blocked the light from the living room, something on the wall caught my attention. There, as clear as day, were the words "Look Here," written in fluorescent light, as if written by a child. And, next to the words was an arrow that pointed straight upstairs.

Other faded writing surrounded it—gibberish that I no longer remember. But I'll never forget the cold realization that the arrow pointed to the exact spot where Eleanor had seen the apparition standing, watching over the upstairs hallway.

Suddenly, the lamp and the dollhouse didn't feel so innocent anymore.

CHAPTER 33
GINA SESSION 4 CONTINUED

> **Ephesians 6:12** *"For we are not fighting against flesh-and-blood enemies, but against evil rules and authorities of the unseen world, against mighty powers in this dark world, and against evil spirits in the heavenly places."*

Wednesday, September 20, 2023. 2:15 PM

I relayed all of that to Gina—first about the Ouija board, then every last detail about the house in Camarillo.

She paused for a moment before speaking again. "So…," Gina began. "We've been working together for a few weeks, and I'm not sure how to say this, so I'm just going to say it."

This can't be good. Cue the *Fight Club* scene.

"You have a low vibrational entity attached to you, and it goes back to when you were 12. It's been stronger at times, like when you were in your 40s. And I can't get it to release."

I'm sorry, I don't think I heard you correctly. You said a low vibrational what now?

I didn't faint like Jack, the narrator, might have. But suddenly, everything began to make sense.

The stupid Ouija board. The house in Camarillo.

The pointless trips to the ER. The unexplained pain.

The lack of confidence.

The anxiety. The meltdown at my brother's wedding.

The negativity. The bitterness. The hatred.

This entity had been slowly dragging me down, sinking its claws deeper with every passing day. It fed off my negative emotions, clinging to me like a leech, silent and unrelenting. It stopped me from processing the things that had happened to me—from making sense of the chaos in my life. It severed my connections with others, leaving me isolated and raw. It thrived on my shame, the memory of peeing my pants in kindergarten ricocheting endlessly in my mind. It fed on the doubt that twisted its way into my thoughts, on the way I gaslit myself before anyone else had the chance. It applauded when I lost my sh*t at Edward as he sat across from me in the conference room. And it consumed the wreckage left behind when my mood swings came crashing through the floor, leaving me breathless and broken.

It thrived on me, for decades.

We have just lost cabin pressure.

"So... what do I do?" I asked, the shock on my face must have been priceless.

"Well, let me reach out to a friend who specializes in this. Can I text you when I hear back from her?" Gina responded.

"Uh, yeah, that sounds good." I wasn't sure what else to say.

Let me know what your friend says after she gets home from her shift at Ghostbusters HQ.

The call ended, and I went to find my wife. I had no idea what to say or do. This day couldn't get any stranger.

CHAPTER 34

HOW GOD SPEAKS TO YOU

Job 33:14-15 *"For God speaks again and again, though people do not recognize it. He speaks in dreams, in visions of the night, when deep sleep falls on people as they lie in their beds."*

I love escape rooms. Whenever we travel, one of the first things I look for is a highly rated escape room with puzzles we haven't encountered before. The whole family gets involved, and out of the five of us, Tyler has an uncanny ability to remember obscure clues and connect them later in the game. Nora is our designated "code-enterer," if that's even a real term. I'm not saying she doesn't follow the game, but she's always hovering near the lock, ready to punch in the combo as soon as someone calls it out.

I enjoy the organizational aspect. I'm all about ensuring every puzzle gets attention and that everyone plays to their strengths. We've got a pretty impressive winning streak, but the most memorable games are the ones that threw unexpected challenges our way.

One of the best escape rooms we've ever played was in Branson, Missouri. It was a massive hotel setup, complete with a lobby, hallways, and separate rooms. We had to split up just to cover everything, occasionally crossing paths as we each worked through different clues. For most of the game, I had no idea what the others were doing. I was laser-focused, powering through puzzles as fast as I could.

At one point, we got stuck in one of the hotel rooms, and just as we were about to grab the walkie-talkie to ask for a clue, a commercial started playing on the TV—perfectly timed. The clues we needed were hidden right in the middle of the ad. It felt like someone had designed that moment just for us!

We set a time record in Branson, MO. No big deal.

Then there was the room in North Carolina, where we started out as prisoners, handcuffed together, trying to escape and prove our innocence before time ran out. WANTED posters were hidden throughout the room, each with letters that had to be used in a specific order. I must've taken stupid pills that morning, because the order of the letters was obvious, but for the life of me, I couldn't figure out where they needed to go. At one point, I was sitting at a desk with a computer, completely stuck. Tyler walked up, took one look, grabbed the keyboard, and typed in the 12-letter password. Puzzle solved.

We even played a ghost-hunting game after a weekend college visit to Oklahoma State University. There were paintings on the wall in a specific orientation, and we just knew they had something to do with unlocking one of those directional locks. However, we couldn't figure out the exact order of the paintings, so we resorted to brute-forcing the solution: Up/Down/Up/Left/Right.

Nope.

Up/Right/Left/Up/Down.

Nope.

After enough attempts we finally figured it out, though we had no idea how the orientation was actually arranged. Only after the game was over did we realize that we had missed a key piece of information sitting in a desk drawer we never bothered to check. It was probably Nora's job.

The fact is, behind every escape room, there's someone with ultimate control over everything: the game master.

The game master sees it all. They know every clue, every challenge, and how everything fits together. They design the entire room and all the puzzles to test your problem-solving, teamwork, and patience. They understand the layout, the potential pitfalls, and the solutions to every problem a player may encounter. Their ultimate goal is to see you succeed, but they also know that figuring it out is part of the journey.

Before you even step into the room, the game master provides the instructions—rules, guidelines, and everything you need to know. It's all laid out on the website, like a roadmap for what's ahead. You can choose to read it carefully or do what I typically do—skim it and think, "Yeah, yeah, I know the drill."

When you arrive, the game master reviews the basics again: "Don't break anything... Communicate with your team... If you need a clue, just ask." They want you to succeed, but they also want you to work for it. No one walks into an escape room expecting to solve everything in one go. You have to start with the first puzzle, take it one step at a time, and trust that everything will fall into place.

There are well-timed, subtle hints in the room for you to follow. If you can't figure them out, you can always ask out loud, and the game master will respond. I was once in a room where we were so stuck and stubborn about moving forward that the game master came over the walkie-talkie and told us exactly what to do next. She was like, "…put these four numbers into the blue lock on the red door."

We did not tip her that day.

God speaks to us through His word, through Scripture, providing guidelines and instructions for life. Every passage is like a clue—a piece of the puzzle meant to guide us. We don't always see the full picture, but He does.

He doesn't always reveal the final destination right away. You might have to work on the first puzzle before He presents the next one. It's about trusting that each step has a purpose, even when you don't know the whole plan. Just like Nora waits patiently by the lock, ready to enter the 4-digit combo, or how I took job after job that led me to places I didn't necessarily want to go.

Perhaps His word only makes sense later, when you have time to reflect on what it all means. Like how UP/DOWN/LEFT/UP/RIGHT was what we entered, but none of us knew why until the end.[1] Or why Eleanor and I felt so drawn to our house in Texas, not piecing all the parts together until much later.

Sometimes He places a well-timed, subtle hint that demands your attention, like the WANTED posters I just knew meant something. Or like that moment in 2016, sitting in that barn in Camarillo, watching the Christmas Eve service intently through tears streaming down my face, when I knew deep inside that I needed to start believing in something. I saw the hint. I thought I knew what I needed to do. But I didn't follow through.

Sometimes the message comes from someone else, just when you need to hear it. Like the commercial that played in the hotel room in Branson, or when Tyler showed me that I just needed to look at the keyboard to figure out where to place the WANTED poster letters.

Or the fact that someone just told you that you have a low vibrational entity attached to your soul. I didn't realize I needed to hear that. But I did. And I was not sure what to do with that information.

So God was about to pick up the walkie-talkie and say, "Son, the combination is 1-2-3-4-5."

He will get your attention when it's time, and that moment for me was about to happen.

CHAPTER 35
GETTING CLOSER

Luke 15:6 "...Rejoice with me because I have found my lost sheep." *(NIV)*

Wednesday, September 20, 2023. 5:18 PM

I sat around all afternoon waiting for Gina's text. Around 5:00, I drove to join some Academy friends at the soft launch of a brewery a few miles away. The brewery was smack dab in an industrial park, surrounded by a mix of construction companies, dance schools, and the usual small business sprawl.

The owner of Armor Brewery, a West Point grad, shared some mutual connections. I was impressed by the décor as soon as I walked in—a tasteful blend of military memorabilia and rustic charm. For two hours, I anchored myself at the corner of the bar, surrounded by a few acquaintances and some new faces. I spent about an hour chatting with Roxanne, a friend I had met at a networking event in the area, whom I'd invited to hang out so I could introduce her to a few service-academy grads.

Around the two-hour mark, I called it quits. It had been a very long day so far, and there was still more ahead. Roxanne and I walked outside together, continuing our conversation in the parking lot. At some point, the topic veered toward mental health—I don't even remember how it came up. I started telling her a bit about my struggles, and how I had lost it at my brother's wedding, but my mind screamed to unload everything. And I mean EVERYTHING.

Hey, Roxanne, guess what else? Ever have a demon inside you that makes your life suck? Well, this low-vibrational entity is attac….Wait, where are you going?

Yeah, that would be a great way to kill a friendship.

Across the street, I noticed a group of teenagers playing basketball in the parking lot of one of the buildings. For a split second, I wondered why kids would be playing basketball in an industrial park, but I quickly dismissed the thought as I continued my conversation with Roxanne. After a few more minutes, we said our goodbyes, and I made the ten-minute drive home.

Upon arriving home, I found Eleanor in the sitting area adjacent to the kitchen. You might be thinking to yourself, "*Oooh, you have a sitting area. Big shot.*" It's not as fancy as it sounds, but we were proud of what we had created. Over the course of many moves, we never really purchased furniture or decor to fit a specific space; we just made do with what we had, knowing that in another year or two, we'd be off to a different house with a different layout.

There is an open area between the kitchen and the patio door that leads to the backyard. It's large enough for a small table and a couple of chairs, similar to a breakfast nook. Rather than reuse our old, beat up Big Lots pub table that would simply become a catch-all for junk, or rush to IKEA for another bookshelf, we decided to make the most of the space. We found four blue barrel-style chairs that we loved, two end tables that matched the vibe we were aiming for, and then spent weeks searching for the perfect rug that really tied the room together.

For us, this area off the kitchen, in front of a fireplace with light streaming through nearby windows, was a haven for conversation—whether it was just between us or with good friends and family.

Sinking into one of the chairs beside my wife, we continued our earlier conversation, still reeling from the whole "entity" news from Gina. I truly didn't know where to turn, and it felt scary.

After a few minutes of silence, I wondered aloud where the kids were.

"Tyler is out with a friend, Travis is at some church thing, and Nora is upstairs," she replied.

"Huh? Church thing? What do you mean?"

"I don't know. Some friend texted him and asked if he wanted to go to a youth group event tonight," she explained. "He should be back around 9:30."

This was odd, considering our church attendance in recent decades had been limited to weddings and funerals. Other things had always felt more pressing, like watching the Eagles on Sunday, going grocery shopping, or anything other than going to church.

In any case, I didn't think much of it, and we continued talking for another hour or so. But ultimately, all I could do was wait to hear back from Gina about the next steps. Maybe her friend was still wrapping up a demon detox session and would be back soon.

Sleep was not in the cards for me that night. Sometime around midnight, hours after Eleanor had fallen asleep, I reached for my iPad and turned to the World Wide Web. I began searching for "low vibrational entity." As it turns out, a lot has been written about that topic, including reputable scholarly research platforms like TikTok, Quora, and Reddit.

Great. Now I have that in my search history.

Next, I began searching for "churches near me that do exorcisms" and "exorcists near me." In case you were wondering, churches don't list "exorcisms" among their services on their '*About Us*' page. However, I did find a Catholic church that outlined steps to request an appointment with a local parish priest. Helpful—if I happened to live anywhere near Washington, DC, where the church was located.

Then, out of nowhere, I had a revelation—a thought that suddenly popped into my mind: Travis was at a church earlier tonight, what about that place? I pulled up Life 360 on my phone, one of those apps that lets you track everybody's whereabouts, to see where he was.

Holy crap. There's no way this can be a coincidence. He was at a place called City Point Church, just 100 yards across the street from Armor Brewery.

Earlier that evening, as I stood outside Armor talking to Roxanne, I unknowingly saw my son across the parking lot, playing basketball with friends as the sun dipped below the horizon. He had been dropped off at 6:26 PM to attend a youth service he had never been to before—sixty-eight minutes after I arrived at the brewery.

God put me exactly where I needed to be, guiding me through every stage and preparing me to solve life's puzzles.

He surrounded me with a loving family who taught me hard work, discipline, and grace.

He also put me in front of people like Coach Nunamaker and Coach Robinson so that I could build the mental tenacity to carry me through the toughest of times.

He brought Eleanor and me together in the same space and time in that food court in Norfolk so that years later we would partner and walk through the peaks and valleys of life.

He steered me in the right direction throughout my career: NFO instead of pilot, E-2s over jets, California instead of Norfolk, Germany instead of Florida, turning down the aircraft carrier pipeline, and choosing Dallas when our life was settled in Virginia. On and on it goes.

And then, while He was preparing me, He was speaking to me the entire time. He provided little hints and nudges along the way.

Like that time on deployment when my roommate Suede asked what I would do if I saw someone drowning in a pool. He was extending his hand, but I scoffed at him.

Like when I sat in the barn in Camarillo during the Christmas service, bawling my eyes out because I knew in my heart that God was calling me. But I let a voice tell me that we were too busy.

Like when He led us to a house with issues in the foundation—the very thing that supports the entire load and withstands all harsh conditions—only to realize that it could be healed.

He had done all these things for me, yet I was still struggling to put all the pieces and clues together. I was staring at the lock but didn't know the combination that would set me free. So now it was time to bring out the walkie-talkie, because now I had a hint I couldn't possibly ignore.

One hundred yards separated me from the darkness I battled and the light I didn't yet recognize. God had placed me exactly where I needed to be.

We have regained cabin pressure.

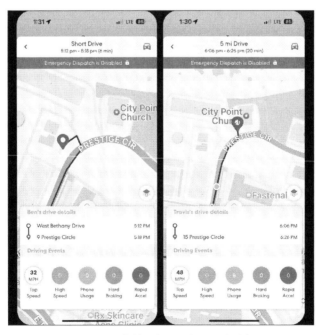

My location (left) and Travis' location (right)

PART FOUR
SAVED

Revelation **3:20** *"Here I am! I stand at the door and knock. If anyone hears my voice and opens the door, I will come in and eat with that person, and they with me." (NIV)*

CHAPTER 36
A DESPERATE SEARCH

Matthew 7:7 *"Ask, and it will be given to you; seek, and you will find; knock, and it will be opened to you."*

Thursday, September 21, 2023. 9:00 AM

Now that I had zeroed in on a church, it was time for some in-depth research. Over-researching is one of my strengths (according to me), and also (according to my wife) one of the things that drives her up a wall.

If you're buying a mattress, a car, or even a countertop ice maker, you need a spreadsheet that outlines the pros and cons of each option. It's just what you do. You wouldn't simply walk into a store and say, "That one!"—that would be crazy.

In any case, as the night stretched on, I scoured the church's website and social media accounts. I tried to find anything I could about the pastors – Facebook, LinkedIn, anything. Maybe, illogically, I was hoping to see a post that said "Helped a guy get rid of his demons last weekend! #devilbegone #GodIsGreat!"

Disappointed, the only information I could find was the church's opening hours: 9:00 a.m. At least I had a starting plan and a bit of relief, and I think I finally crashed around 3 or 4 a.m.

I was awake a few hours later, and as dawn broke, I debated waking my wife to tell her what I'd found.

The second she started to stir, I was all over her, sharing everything I had found. "Will you come with me this morning?"

"What are you going to say?" she asked.

"I don't know yet," I replied, "but I'll figure something out."

I actually did have the question phrased in my head already, and I kept practicing over and over to make it sound somewhat "normal." I had to say just the right thing; otherwise, a door might get slammed in my face. So I couldn't just say, "Hey, I've got a demon inside my body. Can you help?"

The kids all left for school—a combination of driving, bussing, and walking for the three of them. By 8:45 a.m., Eleanor and I were in the car, my nerves churning. We arrived at the church at 8:55, where a single truck sat in the parking lot. After waiting for a few minutes, we walked up to the front door at 9:00 sharp and rang the doorbell. It was still dark inside, giving the impression that nobody had shown up for work that day. We knocked a couple of times, but no one came to answer.

Let's go get coffee or something," I said, feeling deflated. "We can come back later."

Eleanor knew in her heart that we were meant to be there, and she told me so right then and there. Months later, she explained the feeling that overcame her as we peered through the dark hallways. It was as if God was nudging her to continue so that she could bring me to Him.

"Someone's here; there's a truck in the parking lot," she pointed out. "Let's try the back door."

We walked around the side of the building and found a glass door leading to a dimly lit hallway. I pressed the buzzer, and the silence stretched into an eternity. Finally, a man in his early forties, clad in a T-shirt and jeans, tattoos peeking out, answered. He opened the door, a hint of suspicion on his face. "Hey, how can I help y'all?" he asked, still blocking the entrance slightly.

"Hi. Is there any way we can speak with one of the pastors?" I managed to say despite my nerves.

"Actually," he replied, "I'm the operations pastor. And I'm also a certified marriage counselor."

I chuckled inwardly. Was he mistaking us for a troubled couple? I suppose that would make sense. With my next sentence, I felt like I had only one chance to get it right.

"It's not that, actually. I'm not sure how to ask this, so if it sounds crazy, maybe you can just say a prayer for us, and we'll go. But does the church believe in low vibrational entities? And that they can take over someone's soul?

A subtle shift crossed his face. "Ummm…" He glanced at his watch. "Come in," he said. "Let's go grab some coffee and talk inside."

CHAPTER 37
SAVED BY THE BELL

Romans 10:9 "If you openly declare that Jesus is Lord and believe in your heart that God raised him from the dead, you will be saved."

Thursday, September 21, 2023. 9:05 AM

T he air conditioner in the dimly lit room was on full blast, and drips of condensation fell from the ceiling, landing on the black leather sofa where my wife sat. Pastor Stephen was next to Eleanor on the other end of the sofa, waiting for me to continue. My wife hadn't said a word in over five minutes—not since she convinced me not to give up and go home. The room carried a distinct "church" aroma— reminiscent of walking into a Marriott lobby, with that clean, slightly luxurious blend of fresh linen and subtle citrus. But instead of calming me, it intensified the pounding in my head.

The imaginary devil in the red suit was practically shouting into my right ear.

You know how crazy you sound, right? Just leave. Just say 'sorry, I made a mistake' and walk out the door.

What if that little guy was right? I'd been to the ER so many times, only to be told I was fine. I'd sat across from counselors who either handed me pills or suggested bubble baths and walks, as though my soul could be repaired by lavender and Epsom salt. Now, here I was again, laying my vulnerabilities bare to another human—this time with a story so outrageous it barely sounded real. What if Pastor Stephen didn't believe me either?

One more deep breath in... long exhale out...

Suck it up, man. Get a hold of yourself.

I repeated the question that had haunted me for the past 18 hours.

"So, I've had some...things...happen to me recently. And I just need to know if the church believes—or if you believe—that a negative entity can attach itself to someone. And what do you do when that happens?"

Please believe me. Please believe me.

The silence stretched, the question hanging in the air like a fragile glass ornament, ready to shatter. Finally, Pastor Stephen broke it.

"It's funny you ask," he said. "I actually do."

My heartbeat slowed, just a bit.

It wasn't the response I had expected, but it felt like a lifeline tossed into an ocean of confusion and chaos.

"Really?" I whispered. "Maybe I should back up and explain what's been happening."

I laid everything out for him—every embarrassing detail from the past year, every supernatural experience I'd once dismissed as nonsense.

I began with the night of my brother's wedding, nine months earlier. I told him about the counseling sessions. I recounted all my conversations with Gina, shared what I had uncovered about our house, and later, what I had discovered about myself.

I also told him how, just last night, I'd been across the street at the brewery while Travis played basketball with his friends here at this church.

The recounting was exhausting. Reliving this nightmare of my life, especially when part of me still doubted its reality, left me emotionally drained.

A part of me still wanted to stand up, take Eleanor's hand, and walk out before I could be emotionally hurt again. If I had heard the words, "Suck it up, buttercup," I might have completely unraveled.

Thankfully, Pastor Stephen did none of that. Instead, we had one of the most meaningful conversations of my life.

We discussed spiritual warfare—a concept I'd never heard of, despite having known and lived through literal warfare my entire career. He spoke about the presence of the Holy Spirit, the history of fallen angels and Satan, examples of possession from the Bible, and—comfortingly —stories from real-life experiences.

As Pastor Stephen spoke, I started to feel something I hadn't let myself feel in years: hope. Could it be possible that everything I'd been through wasn't just random chaos? Maybe there was something bigger going on?

I wasn't ready to say I had it all figured out—not by a long shot. But for the first time, I started to think that maybe God was real, and maybe He'd been there all along, nudging me toward this moment.

I didn't have a grand epiphany, no lightning bolt of clarity. Just a faint sense that the weight I'd been carrying might not be mine to bear alone. And honestly, that was enough for now.

For the first time in forever, I let myself believe that maybe—just maybe—God was speaking to me. And this time, I was ready to listen.

You've probably heard people say something like, "I got saved when I was [XX] years old." I've heard it countless times throughout my life, and even if I didn't roll my eyes outwardly, I was definitely doing it in my head.

What does that even mean? Don't most people just start going to church when they're kids, hear some stories about a giant wooden boat, a burning bush, or maybe a sea splitting in two?

How do you pinpoint the exact moment when you began a relationship with Jesus? I don't even know the exact moment I "accepted" Eleanor as my wife and best friend.

But I *can* tell you this: just before 10:00 AM, on a Thursday in September, sitting next to Pastor Stephen and holding Eleanor's hand, I asked Jesus to forgive me of my sins. I accepted Him as my Lord and Savior. I promised to follow Him with all my heart.

And as I whispered that prayer, Eleanor's hand tightened around mine. Two souls, caught in the same storm. In that same quiet space, she was making her own surrender. Making the same promises. Finding her own Savior.

And in that moment, in a small green room behind the stage of this church, tucked away in the corner of an industrial park, we passed from spiritual death to spiritual life.

CHAPTER 38
TIME TO CLEAN HOUSE

Acts 16:18 "*This went on day after day until Paul got so exasperated that he turned and said to the demon within her, 'I command you in the name of Jesus Christ to come out of her.' And instantly it left her.*"

Thursday, September 21, 2023. 10:30 AM

As Eleanor and I walked out of the church, Pastor Stephen said, "I've got your number; let me talk to some of the pastors, and I'll give you a call."

We sat in the parking lot for a few minutes before driving off, taking time to process what had just happened. I doubted whether we would actually hear from him. I was already overjoyed that we had barged into someone's workplace and taken up 90 minutes of their time. I was sure he had a million things to do. The last thing I expected was for Stephen to continue "wasting" his time with us. Besides, I felt better already. Wasn't that good enough?

"Wanna go get breakfast?" I asked Eleanor. Since we hadn't eaten yet that morning, the butterflies in my stomach had finally settled, and I needed to replace them with food.

We drove off, searching the map for a place to stop on the way home. About a mile from the church, my phone rang from an unfamiliar number. I wasn't in the mood to talk to a telemarketer or confirm my next doctor's appointment, so I sent it straight to voicemail.

About thirty seconds later, I received a text alert notifying me of a voicemail, and I was shocked to see who it was from. "Hey Ben, this is Pastor Stephen over at City Point," the message read. "It's 10:36 right now. I just wanted to call and see—we actually have some availability. If you guys are at home or can be at home, we can head over there in just a few. Whenever you get this, give me a call back."

I called him back immediately to give him my address. "What time are you thinking about coming over?" I asked.

"We can be there in about twenty minutes," he said. Well, I guess breakfast will have to wait.

"Sounds great, I'll see you in a few," I responded, hanging up the phone. I turned to Eleanor and said, "He's coming over."

"Who's coming over?" Eleanor asked, giving me that familiar confused look I often receive when I say something out of context.

"Pastor Stephen," I replied, "and he's bringing some others."

"What others?"

"I have absolutely no idea," I said, "but I suppose we should head home because they'll be there in 20 minutes."

No sooner had we pulled into the driveway than the same pickup truck we saw at the church pulled up to the curb. Four people jumped out, walking up the sidewalk to our front door with all sorts of supplies in hand.

If the Ghostbusters' Ectomobile had pulled up and Peter Venkman had knocked on the door with a proton pack, I couldn't have been more shocked.

As we stood on the doorstep, Pastor Stephen introduced everyone. "Okay, y'all, here's what we're going to do. We brought some salt, which symbolizes purity, and we also have anointing oils that we'll apply to the doors and entryways. First, we'll bless the outside of the property, and then we'll come back inside. You can walk with us and pray, or you can hang out until we're finished. It's totally up to you."

"What is happening right now?" I wondered. If my neighbors looked out the window and saw me tossing salt around the perimeter of the house, they'd probably never speak to us again. Part of me wanted to quickly usher them inside to spare myself the trouble of explaining this later.

But Eleanor and I joined them, tossing salt and praying alongside Stephen and the others. Each person held a Bible in one hand and a super-religious blue box of Morton's salt in the other. After ten minutes of walking outside, we moved inside to continue our prayers. The salt was replaced with small vials of oil, which they used to anoint every doorframe and window as they walked through each room.

While all this was happening, I felt a shift in the atmosphere. I can't quite put it into words, except to say that I felt the house grow brighter and less tense. It was as if we had been living in a dark basement with the faint strains of eerie carnival music playing, but now we were outside in the sunshine on a warm spring day, listening to an upbeat playlist. The entire house felt more at ease, more welcoming.

A couple of hours ago, I might have said the simple fact that these religious figures were blessing our home was enough, and all this "brightness" nonsense was just in my head. But I was starting to realize it wasn't. The dark energy that had lingered for decades—clinging to the walls and to me—was being driven out. The shadows were retreating, giving way to the light, and for the first time in years, I could feel it.

After they finished walking every inch of the property, we all gathered in our sitting area—yep, that same sitting area. We continued talking for a couple of minutes, and then Pastor Stephen asked if they could pray with us.

As they gathered around us, placing their hands on our shoulders, Pastor Stephen asked me to think of someone in my life I needed to forgive—someone who had caused me anger, someone who had wronged me, someone I still held a grudge against.

There was a long list to choose from, but I settled on one person in particular, someone I would gladly complain about whenever the opportunity arose. Ever been so angry at someone that you wished they'd wake up, roll out of bed, and leap feet first into an endless sea of Legos? That's how I felt about this guy. Or maybe this girl. Doesn't matter, because I'm not going to tell you who it was.

Pastor Stephen asked me to pray for that person and seek my heart for forgiveness.

While I did that, they all laid their hands on me and began to pray. Stephen led the prayer, but the others joined in, whispering softly to themselves. I heard a lot of "...in the name of Jesus..." being murmured throughout the group.

The weight of the elephant started to lift. I had felt better after leaving City Point, but now I could feel myself physically improving even more. I could feel my chest rise and fall without pain or pressure.

The whispering prayers slowly intensified, sounding like they were coming at me from all directions, as if playing in stereo.

A lone tear ran down my face. The words shifted from praising God and asking for wisdom and knowledge, to speaking directly to evil spirits and demons.

"...I command you, by the power of the Holy Spirit and in the name of Jesus..."

Suddenly, it felt like something was being pulled out from deep inside me.

"...all contracts are broken..."

It was as if a giant, clawed parasite was gripping my inner organs, and with every word spoken in the name of Jesus, that parasite was being torn out. It didn't want to leave—its claws dug in, clinging to whatever they could.

"…cancel any attack…"

I felt the claws slowly begin to loosen. Still trying to hold on to my stomach, my lungs, my heart—but growing lighter and lighter.

"…and place a hedge of protection…"

My nose started to run uncontrollably, but I never once tried to wipe it away or sniff it back. I just let the tears and snot mix together as they streamed down my face.

"…and bring peace to Ben and his family…"

And while their hands were on me, a great peace overcame my entire spirit. Not my body, necessarily, but my spirit. It was an unexplainable calm like I had never felt before. I took a deep breath, feeling lighter.

"…in Jesus' name, Amen…"

Everyone stood silent for a moment. I looked around at the group, wondering if I should speak first.

"You know," I said, turning to Pastor Stephen, "Eleanor and I really did set up this room for a reason, and I believe that reason was today. We were going to put a table in here, but something kept telling me it needed to be a sitting room we could share with others. I believe God brought us together. I don't know if we're meant to be best friends, but there's a reason this is all happening, right here, right now."

In that moment, everything changed.

Everything.

I was finally free.

CHAPTER 39
GOD SPEAKS TO ME

1 Kings 19:12 *"And after the earthquake there was a fire, but the Lord was not in the fire. And after the fire there was the sound of a gentle whisper."*

Thursday, September 21, 2023. 01:15 PM

About an hour after the pastoral team had left our home, I heard God speak to me for the first time.

I was driving my middle son, Travis, to a doctor's appointment. He sat beside me in the truck, his head bent over his phone—standard 13-year-old behavior. Country tunes played softly from my Spotify playlist, but my thoughts were far away, trying to make sense of the whirlwind of the last 24 hours.

I was driving down a busy two-lane road, lost in thought. Out of nowhere, a soft, gentle voice whispered clearly into my left ear:

"You Need to Tell Your Story."

I glanced at Travis to see if he had heard it, but he was still engrossed in a video. The voice felt like it came from just behind me, over my left shoulder, and I turned around (no joke) to check if someone was sitting in the back seat.

As the words settled in, a wave of warmth enveloped me, like being wrapped in a soft blanket. My heart fluttered pleasantly, and a tingling sensation spread through my body, accompanied by a deep peace that washed over me for the third time that day.

I quickly blinked away a tear, wiping it before my son could notice, still grappling with what I had just heard.

What does that mean?

I kept turning those words over in my mind the rest of the afternoon. As soon as I got home, I headed upstairs to my desk and put pen to paper. "Maybe," I thought, "I'm supposed to give a sermon at this new church." I do enjoy public speaking and have had several opportunities to do it throughout my career. But even though we hadn't attended a service yet, could this really be God's plan to put me in front of a room full of strangers?

I spent the next 45 minutes working on a slide presentation that just didn't feel right. It was awkward and forced, like the words wouldn't come together. After about an hour, I set the project aside and headed downstairs, frustrated with myself.

I never heard those exact words from God again, but I never forgot them. In fact, I thought about them almost daily. I considered other ways to share my story, like opening up to close friends about my experiences. Over the next few months, I made a point to open up whenever I sensed someone might be receptive. Most people responded in kind, and a few even broke down, sharing their own struggles. It was healing for both sides, but I still couldn't shake the feeling that I wasn't fully answering God's call.

Nine months after hearing God's voice, the meaning of those words finally became clear to me—though not in the way I expected. What I thought would be a simple task turned out to be something much bigger.

CHAPTER 40
SHOW ME THE MONEY!

Malachi 3:10 *"Bring the whole tithe into the storehouse, that there*
may be food in my house. Test me in this," says the LORD
Almighty, "and see if I will not throw open the floodgates of
heaven and pour out so much blessing that there will not be room
enough to store it." (NIV)

Sunday, September 24, 2023. 9:55 AM

F or most of my life, I thought tithing—the practice of giving a
portion of your income, typically 10%, to support the church—
was completely absurd. I associated it with money-grabbing televange-
lists on TV, guilt-tripping suckers into parting with their hard-earned
cash.

I mean, come on. I'm the one who works for that money. I'm the one
who sacrificed all that time away from home to provide for my family.
Put your hand down, preacher man!

When I was in elementary school, my parents would give me a couple
of dollars to take to Sunday service in Tatamy. I remember how difficult it was to part with that money as the plate passed right in front of
me. Five dollars in the mid-80s could buy a *lot* of candy.

Now, sitting seven rows back at the first church service we'd attended in decades, I couldn't help but cringe when Malachi 3:10 flashed on the screen behind Pastor Eddie, the founder and senior pastor of City Point Church. Just days earlier, I had experienced some of the most unbelievable moments of my life, and I had begun to believe in a higher power. Yet I still didn't want to give my money to a church, especially since I wasn't currently working.

I had a lone $50 bill in my wallet, folded neatly and tucked into an inside divider for emergencies. That bill had probably been there for over ten years.

So, when the donation buckets came around at the end of the service, I faced a decision: give up my trusty emergency $50 bill or look away when the bucket passed by and pretend I didn't see it.

Reluctantly, I shoved the $50 bill into an envelope and dropped it into the bucket.

Great…there goes my trusty emergency $50 bill.

After the service, we walked down the hallway toward the youth rooms to pick up Nora from Club 56, the space for fifth and sixth graders. The hallway and surrounding rooms buzzed with energy.

"Dad!" I heard Nora yell from the back of the room. She came running over, holding a Visa gift card. "I won 50 bucks!"

Stunned, I stared at the card for what felt like an eternity.

Okay, maybe it was just a coincidence. I mean, there were fewer than 10 kids in there, so those were decent odds.

Until it happened again the following week.

After I got home, I reloaded my wallet with another $50 emergency bill. This one was in our safe and was left over from a past birthday card.[1]

I had forgotten about it until the following Sunday, when the bucket was passed around again. "*Dang it!*" I thought. "*I need to start hitting the ATM before church.*"

That Sunday, I put another $50 bill into the collection bucket.

And that Sunday, Nora walked away with another $50 gift card, having won a game where they had to memorize Bible verses.

God was nudging me along, revealing that I could trust in Him. Maybe the "emergency $50 bills" were meant to help me?

After two striking 'coincidences' involving money exchanged between us and the church, you'd think we'd be convinced. You'd think I'd see Malachi 3:10 in a whole new light. As the weeks went by, we gradually increased our giving. But because we were still wrestling with doubts about how much was enough—or whether we could truly trust God with our finances—we didn't fully commit to tithing in the traditional sense.

Later that fall, City Point launched a campaign called "Believe" to raise funds for a larger facility better suited to the growing congregation.

"Go home and pray over it," Pastor Eddie said during a November Sunday service. "We're hoping to raise enough over the next three years so we'll be ready for whatever God has in store for us."

Something about the campaign tugged at my heart. I brought up the topic to my wife afterward, and her shrug of the shoulders made it clear this wasn't a topic to pursue right now.

Still, I prayed about it, and I think she did too. A few weeks later, I broached the subject again. By that point, we had decided to call City Point our home. I shared the dollar amount I had in mind, where we could get the money, and suggested that instead of spreading it out over three years, we give it all at once.

She agreed.

The next day, I entered my bank account information into the payment portal and hit submit on the largest donation I'd ever made in my life. It felt pretty good.

That afternoon, as I walked back from the mailbox with piles of magazines, advertisements, and other junk mail, I spotted an envelope from our mortgage company. *Interesting, what do they want now?*

Inside was a refund check from our escrow account. It more than covered the amount I had sent to City Point that morning.

I thought about all the paychecks that had come in over the years, and how I had the U.S. government and taxpayers to thank for providing a good life for my family. I never stopped to think that God was providing for us. And, sharing His blessings with others had never even crossed my mind. I would even cringe when I saw that guy dressed up as Santa Claus outside the grocery store every Christmas, ringing that annoying bell and asking for change. I'd just look away and avoid him.

At the age of 47, I finally realized I didn't even control my finances. And it wasn't the government, either. I was merely a steward of God's blessings.

Yep.

CHAPTER 41
GOD SPEAKS AGAIN

> **Isaiah 40:26** *"Lift up your eyes and look to the heavens: Who created all these? He who brings out the starry host one by one and calls forth each of them by name. Because of his great power and mighty strength, not one of them is missing."*

Tuesday, September 26, 2023. 5:10 PM

Two days after our first church service at City Point, I had another scheduled session with Gina. It had been nearly a week since our last conversation, and while Eleanor had texted her a few days earlier to mention we'd visited a church, she didn't know all the details.

"So, let me tell you about what happened after our session last week," I began. I recapped everything—from Travis joining the youth group to my research about the church, knocking on the door and meeting Pastor Stephen, the visit from the pastoral team to our house, and even hearing God's voice while I was driving.

"Wow," she finally managed. "That's amazing. And how do you feel now?"

"I feel absolutely amazing. Like I've been set free," I said.

As we continued, she checked for any negative energy that might still be affecting me.

"It looks like that low vibrational energy is gone. This is so incredible! I'm glad this worked out for you guys. And I've checked the house; I'm not seeing anything there either," she continued. "So, what would you like to work on today?"

Then, just like Friday morning when I was driving with Travis, the same voice whispered over my left shoulder:

"Tell her that I've got you now."

"Ummm….well." I stalled, trying to grasp what was happening. My eyes filled with tears, and I looked down at my hands, searching for the right words. I had spent my entire life in spiritual silence, and now, I was hearing God's voice as clearly as if He were right beside me.

"Gina, you know I appreciate you and everything that you've done. And I don't mean this in a bad way at all. But I think God needed to use you to bring me to Him. Because I just heard Him say *'Tell her that I've got you now.'*"

I didn't try and fight the tears, they just flowed. She welled up too, and we both sat there in silence, too stunned to know what to say next.

I spoke up first. "So, I guess this means I don't really need these sessions anymore. I think we're done."

We continued talking for a few minutes, then wrapped up the session early.

PART FIVE
REACHING OTHERS

Matthew **28:19-20** *"Therefore, go and make disciples of all the nations, baptizing them in the name of the Father and the Son and the Holy Spirit. Teach these new disciples to obey all the commands I have given you. And be sure of this: I am with you always, even to the end of the age."*

CHAPTER 42
INTRO TO WALLY

Romans 12:2 *"Do not conform to the pattern of this world, but be transformed by the renewing of your mind. Then you will be able to test and approve what God's will is—his good, pleasing and perfect will."*

Sunday, October 15, 2023. 9:00 AM

On a brisk fall morning, we headed into the 9:00 AM service at City Point. It had been less than a month since we first walked through those doors. This Sunday was different—Pastor Eddie wouldn't be giving his usual sermon. Instead, a special guest was there to speak: Pastor Wally Cook.

Pastor Wally was visiting from El Salvador on his annual U.S. trip, ready to share his inspiring story about going from hippie to missionary.

In 2003, Wally and his wife, Judy, left their roles as youth pastors at Word of Victory Outreach Center in Canton, Texas, to start Amazing Love Missions (ALM). El Salvador became their new home, and they've dedicated themselves to that community ever since.

ALM does some pretty amazing things. They run English language schools that help locals secure jobs in English-speaking industries, such as call centers and airports. They also provide feeding programs in impoverished neighborhoods and offer scholarships, giving young people the opportunity to attend college or trade schools, breaking the cycle of poverty.

One of their key initiatives is Tia Ana's Shelter, which offers children from broken homes a safe, nurturing place to grow up.

In 2013, they founded the Earthquake School of Supernatural Ministry, helping students deepen their faith, learn to hear God's voice, and prepare to share the love of Jesus in transformative ways.

ALM also hosts mission teams from the U.S. who come to teach, participate in feeding programs, and offer healing services. It's all about building up the community and transforming lives—both theirs and ours.

Though I didn't realize it at the time, seeds were being planted as Pastor Wally took the stage that Sunday morning.

"Before we get started," he began, his Texas drawl evident. "I wanna do something that the Lord asked me to do even before I left El Salvador… In just a minute I'm going to ask everybody under the age of 25 to stand, and here's why: When they do that, the rest of us are going to do a prophetic act and we're going to applaud for them…I believe the Lord wants them to know that heaven applauds them."

He went on to share his experience of being saved 50 years ago. He was just a guy with long hair, playing in a rock band, and when he was saved, he shifted from being part of the counterculture to being embraced by the mainstream.

"Our young people today," he continued, "…it's the other way around. When they get saved, they go from being embraced by the predominant culture to being IN the counterculture. They pay a bigger cost. It costs them more to follow Jesus than it did for me 50 years ago." [1]

Take a moment to think about that. Reread it if you need to. Today's

Christians face a unique challenge: following Jesus often feels counter-cultural, demanding both courage and conviction.

"Heaven applauds you. Heaven honors you," Pastor Wally repeated, as a group of teens and young adults stood to be recognized. As the applause filled the auditorium, something clicked. It felt like the Holy Spirit had inspired Wally to speak directly to me, knowing I needed that encouragement.

In just a few weeks, I had changed so much. I went from simply going through the motions to fully submitting to a higher power. How would my friends and family react? Could I really share this newfound faith openly? How would I even bring it up?

Heaven truly does cheer for those who choose a different path, and honestly, it wasn't a path I would have imagined just a few months earlier.

CHAPTER 43
HEADED SOUTH

Acts 1:8 *"But you will receive power when the Holy Spirit comes upon you. And you will be my witnesses, telling people about me everywhere—in Jerusalem, throughout Judea, in Samaria, and to the ends of the earth."*

Saturday, June 22, 2024. 7:00 AM

By 7:00 AM, nervous excitement filled the lobby at City Point Church. We all arrived within about five minutes of each other, luggage in hand, ready to head to the airport for an eight-day mission trip to El Salvador. Our group of fifteen was a mix of mission trip veterans and wide-eyed novices like me, and I had no idea what to expect.

As we gathered, I couldn't help but think back to how it all started. Months earlier, during a casual lunch with Pastor Stephen, he mentioned his upcoming trip to El Salvador, and I wasted no time asking my share of clueless questions.

"You're going to El Salvador?" I asked. "For vacation?"

"No, man, I'm taking a team down for a mission trip. Remember Wally, the guy who preached at City Point a few months back? We've been working with him for years. He's our host and point man when we get down there. I've been coordinating all the logistics and setting up the schedule with him."

I thought back to my time traveling abroad. When U.S. Navy ships docked in foreign ports, there were often opportunities to do community service—cleaning up trash or visiting retirement homes for a couple of hours. I never got involved; I was more focused on drinking and playing golf. I assumed these church mission trips were similar: maybe we'd help build a house, or visit an orphanage to hand out water bottles and toys while sprinkling in some scripture quoting—like Oprah handing out her favorite things. "YOU get some JESUS, and YOU get some JESUS!"

"So, on these trips, do you like... build things?" I asked, genuinely curious.

Pastor Stephen chuckled, clearly amused by my naivety.

"No, we go down to minister to the people. We attend church services, pray with them for healing, worship together—stuff like that. We also spend time with Tia Ana and her kids at the orphanage. We visit English language schools and work with adults learning to speak English. You should consider coming. It's a pretty life-changing experience."

"*Life Changing?*" I scoffed to myself. I've used that phrase so much, I'm not even sure what it really means anymore. I mean, I consider the burnt ends at Hutchins BBQ in McKinney, TX to be 'life-changing.' But what did it really mean in the context of a mission trip?

I'd traveled to over 40 countries while in the Navy, and we'd even lived in Germany for a few years. Navigating foreign lands, handling language barriers, and haggling in souvenir markets were second nature to me. El Salvador sounded like just another trip—another Starbucks City mug to add to the collection.

Over the next few days, God nudged me in ways I couldn't ignore. I couldn't stop thinking about all my past travels and how they had been entirely self-serving: finding a nice hotel, the best restaurants, and where I could play golf next. Maybe this was my chance to do something different, something meaningful for someone else.

What started as a casual conversation at a Mexican restaurant quickly transformed into a calling. I reached out to Stephen, and just like that, I was added to the list.

I t was during our first group meeting on February 25th that the trip began to take shape for me. We were an eclectic mix, ranging from teenagers to people in their 60s. Some had mission trip experience, and some of us were first-timers. We met monthly before the trip to cover logistics and prepare for what lay ahead.

We received handouts outlining the dos and don'ts for the trip and signed release forms, promising to behave and stay out of trouble. I vowed to a) not return with a suitcase full of cigars and b) limit my intake of Salvadoran beer. We were also given a copy of Pastor Wally's e-book, *Healing is Easy?* to help us prepare for the week. It's a quick, straightforward read that discusses the incredible healing works Jesus has performed.[1]

One Sunday afternoon, Pastor John, one of our church pastors, talked to us about spiritual warfare. "God is planning to use each of you on this trip to reach others," Pastor John said, looking each of us in the eye. "The enemy will try to sow seeds of doubt. There might be travel delays. You'll get tired. You might get frustrated with some of the other team members," he continued. "All those things are meant to distract you from what God has planned."

This feels like a bit of a stretch. Is the devil really in charge of travel delays? Isn't this just an excuse for people to complain about their problems?

As the trip approached, I kept hearing the same message from everyone I spoke with: 'Prepare for life-changing, supernatural experiences.'

There are, of course, moments that reshape us—events that change the trajectory of our lives and shift our perspectives. Like that hot summer day in 1994 when I raised my hand and swore an oath to the Constitution. Or ten years later, on a perfect October day in 2004, when Eleanor and I said, "I do" to each other. Or when I watched Tyler's birth in 2007, followed by Travis a couple of years later in 2009. And then, in 2013, when the nurse held up Nora and said, "Euer Mädchen ist hier."

These were defining moments, the ones that created a new version of me. But a trip to another country? How could that possibly change my life? I'm not even friends with anyone on this trip, not like when I was pulling into foreign ports with my Navy buddies. So, call me skeptical about this whole 'life-changing event' idea.

Yes, I know. You'd think by now I would've learned.

That seed planted by Wally's message last October had begun to bear fruit, and now, here I was—bags packed, ready to embark on something that felt equal parts thrilling for its newness and terrifying for its unknowns.

As we loaded our bags into the church shuttle bus that morning, everyone was excited to get this trip underway. With 15 people on the team, some of us (myself included) packed as if we were leaving for six months. There was no way all our bags were going to fit in the shuttle, so one of the spouses volunteered to follow in her SUV.

We stuffed suitcase after suitcase into the shuttle and SUV, trying every possible configuration to fit the mountain of luggage. Pastor Julie, Pastor Eddie's wife, was running late—not by a couple of minutes, but by a full 30. Just when we thought we had everything packed, we had to rearrange it all to squeeze in two more bags.

Of course, we had to take a group picture in our church-issued shirts (don't you always?). Unfortunately, mine was buried at the bottom of my suitcase, so I spent a frustrating 10 minutes digging it out from the bottom of the stack. I was starting to sweat, and my patience was wearing thin.

Token "goofy" photo before loading up the shuttle

After 45 minutes of wrangling logistics and hashing out last-minute plans, we finally loaded up and hit the road. But in the blistering Texas heat, our church shuttle bus quickly turned into a sauna—none of us could figure out how to turn off the floor heaters. What started as a light-hearted, laughter-filled morning quickly shifted as the jokes about the heat gave way to rising frustration. Maybe there really is something to this whole "Satan messing with travel plans" thing.

Luckily, the rest of the drive and flight went off without a hitch. On the way to San Salvador, I found myself sitting next to two guys from Eastern Tennessee who were heading down on a mission trip with their church. One of them, a dentist, planned to provide dental care for the locals all week.

"Do you have any doctors with your group?" he asked.

"No, nothing like that," I said.

"Oh? So what will you guys be doing?"

I hesitated, unsure how to answer, and vaguely mentioned something about visiting local churches and spending time at an orphanage.

The look on his face reflected the same uncertainty I was feeling: *"What exactly are we going to be doing down here?"*

The flight flew by, and about three and a half hours later, we touched down in San Salvador. After disembarking, we headed to baggage claim to retrieve what felt like 40,000 pounds of luggage. A brief wave of panic hit when three bags didn't show up on the belt, but after 20 nerve-wracking minutes, everything turned up.

Once outside, we were greeted by Pastor Wally, our host for the week, and Jimmy, our ever-reliable driver. Hugs went around for those who had been before, and introductions followed for the newcomers. We shuffled toward the parked shuttle as Jimmy sized up the mountain of luggage, mentally solving the 3-D jigsaw puzzle we had just tackled back home a few hours ago.

As we drove to the hotel, I felt a weird mix of nerves and excitement building. This was it—the start of something completely different, and honestly, I had no idea what to expect. The lush green landscape outside the window was a far cry from the dry plains of Northern Texas, and for the first time, it hit me that this wasn't just another trip. This was something bigger.

I looked around at the team. Some people were laughing and chatting like they'd known each other forever, while others sat quietly, probably lost in their thoughts about what the week might bring. Me? I was somewhere in between—eager to see what God had in store but still unsure how I'd fit into it all.

Whatever was coming, I figured I'd just have to take it as it came. El Salvador was waiting, and I was about to see firsthand how God works through people—even skeptics like me.

CHAPTER 44
THE FIRST DAY IN EL SALVADOR

> *Proverbs 1:8-9* *"My child, listen when your father corrects you. Don't neglect your mother's instruction. What you learn from them will crown you with grace and be a chain of honor around your neck."*

Sunday, June 23, 2024. 7:45 AM

That first morning at the hotel, as I sat down for breakfast, I had no idea what the day had in store. I certainly didn't expect to be crying uncontrollably just a few hours later, all because of music.

And I definitely didn't expect to fall in love with Salvadoran breakfast. Huevos rancheros, a variety of beans, fried plantains, vibrant sausages, an assortment of cheeses, and even homemade salsa filled the table. I left completely stuffed, not missing the sad, soggy scrambled eggs and microwaved bacon served at most American hotel chains.

The only thing missing from the meal was pupusas—thick cornmeal flatbreads stuffed with cheese or beans, served with a tangy red salsa and fermented cabbage slaw. Absolutely delicious. After trying them for the first time on the way from the airport, I knew I'd be having plenty more before the trip was over.

After a hearty breakfast, we piled into the shuttle and headed to Encounter Church, a modest gathering space tucked inside an office building in downtown San Salvador. Glancing at the schedule, I saw we had a 9:00 AM service, but this setup wasn't what I had envisioned. Escorted through security, we took the elevator to the upper floors. As the doors opened, we walked down a narrow hallway lined with Spanish office signs and photos before reaching the double doors that marked the entrance to "the church."

The space served as a cafeteria during the week, with tables and chairs pushed aside on Sundays to make room for the congregation. This was Pastor Wally's home church, and he clearly knew everyone well. We were greeted with warmth and smiles as we stepped inside.

Arriving a few minutes early, some of our group used the time to rehearse the two worship songs they'd perform throughout the week. Pastor Julie led with vocals, while Pastor Stephen and Brian played guitar and sang. Liz was on the keyboard, Wally handled the bass, and a member of Encounter provided percussion using a large wooden box that doubled as drums.

As the locals began to fill the small cafeteria, they greeted one another with kisses and found seats in the orange plastic chairs. The service opened with the Encounter Church worship team, and instantly, the room was no longer a cafeteria but a space filled with the Holy Spirit. Though the songs were sung entirely in Spanish—a language I didn't understand—the powerful, soul-stirring music dissolved any language barrier. As the music filled the space, tears started to stream down my cheeks. I didn't try to stop them; I just let them flow, attempting to follow along with the Spanish lyrics displayed on a TV in the corner.

After a few songs, the City Point worship team was introduced, and our members stepped forward to grab their instruments. Pastor Stephen began with a Spanish worship song called *Tu Amor Nunca Falla*, meaning *Your Love Never Fails*. Hands were raised, hips swayed, and the congregation sang every line with heartfelt joy.

The emotion and devotion in the room was intense. I noticed a man in the corner, visibly filled with the Holy Spirit, having a loud conversation with someone who wasn't physically there. Two women to my left spent the entire service prostrate on the floor, deep in prayer. For 45 minutes, I was completely overwhelmed by the Holy Spirit's presence. It was a profound spiritual encounter, and I began to understand why the church was named "Encounter."

Pastor Stephen and Pastor Julie leading Worship at Encounter Church

Pastor Juan, the lead pastor, then took the stage for the sermon, accompanied by a translator to help us Americans follow along. His message centered on integrity, and he shared a personal story about the importance of honesty, even in the small things. He recalled a time when he was undercharged for several items at a store. After realizing the mistake, he chose to go back and pay the correct amount. His decision left the store staff baffled—they couldn't understand why someone would return just to pay more.

As Pastor Juan spoke, each word felt like it pierced straight into my soul. I found myself reflecting on moments in my life when I chose silence instead of speaking up. Once again, God was speaking to me—

but this time, it was through Pastor Juan's message, urging me to confront my own values and decisions.

After Pastor Juan finished, we were invited to the front to pray with church members who needed support.

In preparation for this trip, we had been required to serve on the altar/prayer team during a few services to get comfortable with strangers approaching us for prayer. I completed my five services, standing beside Pastor John for the first two, watching and learning. In my five sessions, only one person approached me—a teenager asking for prayer before his basketball game.

Now, standing beside Marielos, one of the translators, nervousness crept in. I'd read Pastor Wally's e-book on healing twice, but here I was in a foreign country with limited Spanish, no theology degree, and still hadn't finished reading the entire Bible. My only public prayer experience? That basketball game. If someone asked me to pray for healing from cancer, I had no idea what I'd say.

But for now, I was off the hook. Only two church members came up to me and Marielos: one asked for prayer for her job, and the other for general health. Phew—easy enough.

Afterward, while standing in a circle with some of the translators guiding us that week, Marielos pulled me aside. She was easily 20 years younger than me, yet here she was, confidently stepping into a mentor role. With a serene yet intense expression, she locked eyes with me and delivered a message in perfect English that resonated through every fiber of my being: "I feel God wants you to know that you're going to be a cornerstone and change someone's life," she said earnestly. "Even if what you have to say is embarrassing, it's okay to share it."

Immediately, I thought about God speaking those same words to me last year: *"You need to tell your story."* It seemed I now had a better roadmap for what this week would bring.

CHAPTER 45
UNDERSTAND GOD'S GIFTS

John 10:27 "My sheep hear my voice, and I know them, and they follow me."

E very year, as part of our Navy physical, we had to take a hearing test. If you've never experienced one of these, let me paint the picture. There's a small soundproof booth with padded walls and carpeted floors, sealed tightly with a heavy door. Inside, there are usually 8 to 10 hard plastic stools designed to be as uncomfortable as possible. The lighting is dim enough to encourage a nap, but those stools make sure that's not happening.

Outside the booth, the corpsman waits for everyone to check in, which always takes longer than it should. The audiologist assigns each person a seat, and one by one, ten or so people shuffle in, grab the headphones, and make sure the blue part goes on the left ear and the red on the right. Or maybe it's the other way around. It's been a while.

It's dead silent in the booth. You can hear every breath. You can even hear your eyelashes slamming together with every blink. If an elderly spider were to crawl across the floor, you'd hear all 48 of his joints pop, and could probably distinguish between his feet hitting the carpet fibers and the cane that he carried. It's really quiet in there. [1]

After what feels like an hour, an audio recording finally begins:

"This is a hearing check. You will be listening for some tones. When you hear a tone, press the button once and quickly release the button. No matter how faint the tone, press the button when you hear a tone and quickly release the button. Upon completion of your hearing check, please remain seated and quiet until the operator releases you."[2]

The guy's voice is soooooo soothing. He really makes you want to try your hardest, and if I ever get to meet him, I'm inviting him over to read me a bedtime story.

Then, you wait for the tones to begin. The low tone is always first, sounding like a tugboat horn playing from 15 miles away.

Was that a tone? Maybe?

Meanwhile, the guy next to you decides that his emphysema cough can't wait any longer.

Great, there goes 25 seconds I can't get back.

Next comes the high-frequency tones, like a high-pitched whistle being softly blown by a mosquito.

Of course, the other nine people have decided that they need to shift their stools around, but not at the same time. They each take a full 10 seconds, sequentially, adding another 90 seconds of commotion.

After getting a few tones right, my mind starts to wander, thinking about the 45 things that I need to do that day.

Then after lunch, I have a 1:00 meeting with… crap! Did I miss another one?

With all the distractions in the booth, it's hard to hear those tiny little tones. It takes laser focus and concentration, and honestly a little bit of practice.

Now imagine how much harder it would be if you didn't know tones were playing around you at all. Picture a random Tuesday at work: you're buried in emails, the phone won't stop ringing, and Kathy in the next cubicle won't shut up about her neighbor's trash cans. If a strange guy in a lab coat suddenly walked up to you and asked, "Did you hear that?" you'd probably respond, "Hear what?" or, more likely, "Who the hell are you?"

But the more times you take the test, the more familiar you become with those faint tones. You start to recognize the pattern, anticipate when they'll hit your ears, and tune out the distractions.

With the distractions of daily life and the constant noise around us, recognizing God's voice can feel as challenging as hearing those faint tones in the hearing test. But as we were about to learn, listening isn't just about silence—it's about tuning in and being intentional.

That afternoon, while gathered in the backyard of Wally's home in San Salvador, we sat in lawn chairs, eating sandwiches and snacking on the Salvadoran versions of Cheetos and Doritos, fully engaged as Pastor Juan and Pastor Wally taught us how God can use ordinary people to heal others and deliver prophetic words.

But first, we needed to hear what He sounds like.

CHAPTER 46
I DON'T KNOW ... BLUE?

1 Corinthians 2:10 *"But it was to us that God revealed these things by his Spirit. For his Spirit searches out everything and shows us God's deep secrets."*

Sunday, June 23, 2024. 12:30 PM

"What color does this person represent, and why?"

These were the words exchanged as we sat across the table in Wally's backyard, having just arrived at his home in San Salvador to discuss the week ahead. Pastor Wally had handed the floor over to Pastor Juan, who began teaching us how to listen to and discern God's messages.

"Jesus made the supernatural possible," Pastor Juan explained. "We all hear God in different ways—some through voices, others through dreams or visions. But all we need to do is ask God what He thinks, then give some space to hear His response."

"We're going to try an exercise. I want everyone to face the person across the table, clear your head, and say the first thing that comes to mind when you ask this question."

Facing the person across from me, I asked aloud, "What color does he represent and why?" Initially, there was nothing; I guess I thought of the color blue. But what did it represent? Royalty, maybe? I wasn't sure.

"Why does this work for everyone else but not for me?" I wondered, feeling a bit foolish as the word "royalty" escaped my lips. Maybe this isn't real, or maybe it is, but God doesn't want to speak to me this way.

Moving to the next exercise, Pastor Juan said "Ok, let's try another one. Let's switch partners." After a quick game of musical chairs, I found myself sitting across from Pastor Stephen.

"Ready?" Pastor Juan continued after we were seated. "Ask this question: What animal does this person represent and why?"

I turned to Stephen and asked, "God, what animal does Stephen represent, and why?"

Immediately, I pictured a cheetah sprinting across the savannah, outrunning everything around it without looking back. The cheetah needed rest, and when it finally did, a glowing arc of protection formed around it, ensuring it was safe from any threat while vulnerable. I felt strongly, as if the words were unfolding before me, that the Holy Spirit was revealing how Stephen outworked everyone around him—and he knew it. But when it was time for him to rest, something he needed to do more often, he could do so without fear, knowing he was under God's protective watch. I shared all of this with Stephen, who listened intently across from me.

Wow, maybe this isn't so hard after all.

We kept going, taking turns as the questions grew more detailed and the responses deeper. As we got more comfortable with each round, the purpose became clearer. God doesn't need to speak directly into our ears; the Holy Spirit simply reveals something, confirming that it's truly God at work. Maybe God does want to communicate with me this way.

And it wasn't just me—it was working for others in the group too. Each question was asked by both partners, and every answer resonated with me. When I sat across from Jocelyn, a younger girl on the team with a contagious grin, she asked, "God, what are you doing in Ben's life?

Her response was almost immediate. "I see a scene from The Polar Express, where you're going down this huge slide. It's scary because you don't know where it's taking you, but the slide is designed with a purpose, and there's an unseen hand guiding you to a great place. You just have to trust that it'll get you there."

Wow. She didn't know anything about me, but was describing the last nine months of my life—when I had no clue where this spiritual journey was heading. I just had to trust that unseen hand was guiding me.

After an hour of back-and-forth questions, we were starting to get the hang of it. It was clear these exercises weren't just about hearing from God—they were building our confidence in His presence and guidance.

Wally stood up to address our group. "Alright," he began, "now that you've seen how God speaks to each of us in different ways, it's time to talk about prayer and healing. Remember, there are over thirty healing miracles in the New Testament, and they all have one thing in common: they're short, direct prayers aimed at the problem."

I thought back to Pastor Wally's book and how the Bible showed us why this would work:

> When Jesus sent out the 12 (disciples) and later the 72, He did 3 things to equip them before He sent them out. First, He taught them. The whole healing class basically was that He had given them authority over every sickness and disease. That was all that they needed to know to be successful.
>
> He also gave them experience. Before they prayed for their first sick person, they had already seen thousands, if not tens of thousands of people healed. They knew beyond a shadow of a doubt that healing worked. They expected good things to happen.

The last thing He gave them, and maybe the most important part of their equipping, was affirmation. They knew that He believed in them, and that He had chosen them to go do this. He didn't have any problems with sending them out to heal the sick. He had a plan and they were an integral part of it.[1]

If "ordinary" people in the Bible could lay their hands on others and ask Jesus to heal, maybe it could work for us too. "Sickness go, healing come" quickly became our new mantra.

Wally then asked the group, "Is anyone here experiencing pain right now?" Fifteen hands shot up like it was the most natural thing in the world. He came over to me first. "Where's your pain?" he asked.

"My right knee," I said. The last time I'd tried running on it was almost a year ago, and it still bothered me going up or down stairs.

With a smile, Wally placed his hand on my shoulder. "Jesus is going to mess with you this week, and you're going to like it. This is gonna be good."

He then had one of our group members place a hand on my knee as he said a short, ten-word prayer. The heat from his hand was unmistakable.

Pastor Wally asked, "Move that around and check it out... same, better, or worse?"

"It's way better, and the heat I felt as soon as he touched me..." I responded, astonishment clear in my voice.

But since there was still a bit of pain, he asked, "Can we do it again?"

The second time around, I immediately felt numbness spreading through my knee. But the pain was gone. Instantly.

Pastor Juan teaching (left) and Pastor Wally praying over my knee

"Do you know why that just happened?" Wally asked. "Because Jesus really likes you."

He was right. I had just spent the afternoon witnessing Jesus' love in action, and this was only the beginning.

CHAPTER 47
A NIGHT OF MIRACLES IN A CONCRETE SQUARE

Acts 3:16 *"Through faith in the name of Jesus, this man was healed—and you know how crippled he was before. Faith in Jesus' name has healed him before your very eyes."*

Sunday, June 23, 2024. 5:30 PM

A fter finishing our lesson at Pastor Wally's house, we returned to the hotel for a quick break. We grabbed a bite to eat in the lobby, and by 5:30 PM, it was time to head out again. Jimmy was waiting for us outside, and we piled back into the shuttle, ready for our second church service of the day. This time, we were leaving the city and going to Quezaltepeque, about a 60-minute drive from San Salvador.

As we drove up, Pastor Stephen turned around in the front seat of the shuttle to make an announcement. "Hey y'all, here's what we're going to do tonight. When we get there, I'll pick a few people from our group to go up on stage and ask the Holy Spirit to provide a word for someone in the congregation. This will be after the message, right before we join the prayer team."

Wait… Say that again?

You know that feeling when a teacher writes an impossible math problem on the board, then turns around with chalk (or a marker, depending on your age) and calls on you to solve it? I shrank into my seat for the rest of the drive, hoping the teacher would forget I was even there.

Soon, we left the winding mountain roads and entered a lively town of over 56,000 people. As we drove through the city, we passed open concrete parks alive with activity—markets brimming with colorful goods, people chatting, dogs wandering through the crowd, and kids running freely without a care in the world.

When you hear the word "church," you might picture a building with a steeple, stained glass windows depicting the Last Supper, and a parking lot full of SUVs and minivans. After this morning's service in the office cafeteria, I wasn't sure what to expect anymore, but I had a feeling this place would be different too.

Within minutes, Jimmy, our trusty navigator, expertly steered us down a narrow alley until we arrived at an open-air structure with a corrugated metal roof. Inside, rows of metal folding chairs were set up beneath large speakers hanging from the beams, ready for the evening's service.

The church worship team was already playing, and once again, I found myself singing along to a song I'd never heard before. The pulse of joyful music filled the air, shifting us from observers to active participants in the evening's service.

True to his word, Pastor Stephen selected three members of the group as the service began. When it was their turn, they stepped onto the stage, facing a room full of strangers. Separated by a language barrier as thick as the Central American humidity, they were guided only by the Holy Spirit.

Tia was the first. Pointing to a woman in the crowd, her voice rang with conviction. "God knows something is happening with your marriage, and He sees you as a good wife," she declared. "He wants to be more present in your marriage." I glanced over to see the woman staring at Tia, her eyes wide in disbelief. Her husband, seated beside her, visibly softened and looked down at the floor.

The other two team members shared messages from the Holy Spirit, and a few minutes later, we were called to the front to take prayer requests from the congregation. As I walked up, I passed Tia and asked, "How did you know that about the woman?"

"I don't know," Tia shrugged. "I just knew. It came to me while the music was playing, and I saw the message that God had for her."

Jocelyn and I teamed up with Raul, who was translating for us that night. We had three opportunities to pray with people, and I could never have predicted what was about to happen.

The first woman slowly approached us, and Raul asked, "What is your name?"

"Maria," she said. I didn't need a translation for that one.

"What can we pray for with you?" he asked. As Raul translated, Maria shared that she was suffering from joint pain and battling a thyroid problem, with discomfort in her jaw and neck. As she spoke, I sensed a heavy weight pulling her down. I could feel that something in her family was deeply burdening her. And the intuition was followed by that familiar warm, comforting sensation, and I knew the Holy Spirit was nudging me to share a message.

"I don't know if you're facing challenges in your family, but I feel that God wants you to know He loves you and your entire family," I reassured her, my voice thick with emotion. "He is with you during this crisis—just rely on Him and ask Him for guidance."

She looked up at me, tears brimming in her eyes, and I felt confident that I understood what God's message was for her. More importantly, I felt she understood what that message meant. I asked if we could pray for her, and when she nodded, I gently placed a hand on her shoulder, praying for her joint pain to leave and for healing to come.

The response was immediate. She looked at me, her eyes wide with wonder, and declared that her pain was gone. We continued praying for her thyroid, and Raul added more words, asking for ongoing healing.

Whoa. That was pretty awesome!

As she walked away, a couple approached—the same couple Tia had spoken to just ten minutes earlier. The woman was clearly leading the man, who seemed reluctant, shuffling beside her with his eyes fixed on the ground. She began speaking to Raul, rapidly listing her husband's ailments: diabetes, constant pain and numbness on the left side of his body, and very poor vision. His eyes were completely clouded over, unfocused, staring blankly into the distance.

She went on, explaining to Raul that her husband was suffering from severe depression and had been talking about suicide.

Chills ran down my spine. In that instant, I knew that every struggle and experience, especially over the past 18 months, had prepared me for this moment.

God had brought us together for a reason, and it felt right.

I turned to Jocelyn and asked, "Is it okay if I take this one?" I didn't want to dominate the night since we were all in this as a team.

"Go right ahead," she replied, noticing the smile on my face.

I placed my hand on the man's shoulder and said, "God brought us together for a reason, and I need to tell you that I've struggled with depression too." I paused for Raul to translate, then continued. "But I was healed—not just from the depression, but also from some physical pain—because someone convinced me that Jesus can do anything. So, is it okay if I pray with you?"

He nodded, and I kept my hand on him as I said a quick prayer for his vision. When I finished, I asked him to open his eyes and tell me what he saw. At first, doubt flickered across his face, but as he blinked slowly, he told Raul that his vision was a little better. He did that "meh" gesture, rocking his hand back and forth.

"Alright, let's pray again," I said, channeling my inner Wally. We prayed a second time, and this time, he told Raul his vision had improved to about a 7 out of 10. I smiled and told him, "We're going to do it one more time," and with a small chuckle, added, "The third one's free!"

We prayed a third time, and when his eyes opened, he locked gazes with Jocelyn. "I can see," he whispered, his voice thick with emotion.

Stunned silence.

I had just witnessed a miracle from God. If this was possible, anything was. Tears flowed freely as he embraced us.

"Can we pray for everything else too?" I asked.

This time, Jocelyn stepped in, praying for healing in his mind. When she finished, she turned to the man's wife, gently took her hands, and said, "God sees your unwavering support for your husband. You're doing an amazing job, and He loves you."

As the night went on, we witnessed more instances of healing. A young girl, gently guided by her mother's arm, approached us. In a soft voice, her eyes fixed on the ground as if searching for something unseen, she told us her back had been aching for months.

Just hours after Wally predicted that I would have some fun this week, I burst out laughing like a crazy person. I quickly asked Raul to explain that my laughter wasn't directed at her pain; rather, it was because God had intentionally placed me there for a reason. I shared that I had suffered from similar back pains, which had healed after weeks of persistent prayer. That wasn't entirely true, but I was laughing at the situation. I couldn't tell her that my back had been healed months ago after Gina suggested that trapped energy was the cause of my pain—something that only happened because she mentioned our house was haunted. That would take forever to explain.

In any case, she was healed after the first prayer. Praise Jesus, this was amazing!

Her mother then turned to Raul and told him about her daughter's struggles with anxiety and depression. As Raul translated, I looked into the girl's downcast eyes and saw a reflection of my own past battles. For the second time that night, I shared a piece of my struggles with a stranger. Then we prayed for her healing and invited Jesus into her heart, hoping to share the peace and strength I had found.

As the girl began to walk away, Raul turned to me and said that the Holy Spirit wanted to give her a message about forgiveness. That resonated with me; it was a truth I had learned on my own journey. Letting go of anger and resentment had cleared the way for the clarity I was now experiencing. I watched them take their seats at the back of the church, and I suddenly had a feeling that we weren't finished.

As soon as the service wrapped up, I grabbed Raul and said, "Let's go talk to her again. I think God has more to say." We found her and her mother getting ready to leave, and Raul asked if we could speak with them once more. He turned to me and said, "I won't translate this; it'll take too long, and I think she needs to go soon. I'll fill you in later." I stood beside them and listened, and the message was clear, even for my non-Spanish ears: forgiveness was crucial for her healing. Through tears, she recited a prayer, and I could see the wave of calm wash over her. I didn't know her current situation, but as I left the church to board the bus, I felt a quiet confidence that she would be okay.

The church in Quezaltepeque

CHAPTER 48
NO PAIN

Proverbs 4:22 *"For they bring life to those who find them, and healing to their whole body."*

Monday, June 24, 2024. 5:45 AM

The sun peeked through a crack in the blackout curtains of my third-floor hotel room. It was 5:45 on our second morning in El Salvador, but I had already been up for an hour, waiting for daylight. I quietly slipped on my shoes, careful not to disturb my roommate.

Even if my knee held up, I wasn't sure how far I could go this morning. I was definitely out of shape, but I was eager to give it a try anyway.

I grabbed the hotel key from the small desk in our room and stepped out into the hallway. The hotel was silent; the only person I passed was the young woman at the front desk. I walked outside, turned right, and began a slow jog down Boulevard Luis Poma.

Out of habit, I winced with the first step, expecting pain the moment my running shoe hit the pavement. But there was nothing.

Surprisingly, there were quite a few people on the streets at this hour, heading to bus stops, work, or school. Definitely more than I expected in this city.

So far, so good. I made it about 200 yards, and my right knee was holding up. If this had been last week, I probably would have given up and turned back by now.

After about a quarter of a mile, I turned left, crossing a busy round-about that was starting to see more traffic, and I still felt pretty good. I passed the Coffee Cup, where team members planned to meet up later that morning for their first cup of coffee.

On my right was Price Mart, a warehouse store similar to Costco or Sam's Club. Nearly five minutes in, I was a little winded, but my knee was still holding up. I felt confident.

I passed gated neighborhoods with barbed wire atop 12-foot concrete walls, each with a single entry point guarded by a shack dotted with security cameras. It had been ten minutes.

After about 20 minutes, I found myself back at the hotel. I was pretty out of breath, but for the first time in nearly a year and a half, I finished a run without any pain in my right knee. I couldn't believe it. I grabbed a cup of coffee and went back outside to find a bench where I could watch people walking by on their way to start the day.

I'd say God is pretty good.

CHAPTER 49
HEARTS AND HANDS UNITED: A DAY AT TIA ANA'S

Isaiah 58:10 "*Feed the hungry, and help those in trouble. Then your light will shine out from the darkness, and the darkness around you will be as bright as noon.*"

Monday, June 24, 2024. 9:00 AM

After my first run in what felt like forever, I showered and joined the rest of the team for breakfast. The day was off to a great start, and it was about to get even better as we prepared to visit Tia Ana and the children she had rescued. Tia Ana's home was more than just a shelter; it was a safe haven for children who had endured unimaginable hardships—something we were about to learn much more about.

On our way to her house, Jimmy drove all fifteen of us to a Walmart in San Salvador. Our mission: to create an unforgettable day for a group of children, ranging from 1st grade through high school.

This Walmart could have been anywhere in the world, with its familiar light blue paint and giant white letters welcoming us. The only notice-able difference here was the security fence around the parking lot—a necessary precaution to deter thieves at night.

Once inside, we split into two teams. My group was in charge of gathering party supplies, food, and drinks, while the others picked out toys and gifts. We had just 30 minutes to fill our carts, and we made sure to use every last second of our shopping spree. By the time we were done, we had taken up three full checkout lines—I'm pretty sure the cashiers had never seen so much stuff paid for at once. With the supplies packed in the van, we were ready to set off for the day.

The journey to Tia Ana's was an eye-opener. We started in the crowded chaos of San Salvador, dodging honking cars and weaving through motorbikes on jam-packed city highways. As we left the city behind, the highways turned into winding mountain roads with sharp curves that made you rethink eating breakfast. Eventually, those roads gave way to narrow, uneven local streets that seemed to shrink the farther we went.

When Jimmy made the turn onto what could barely be called a "road" to her house, I couldn't help but think, "We have no business taking this shuttle up the side of a mountain." Yet, he handled it like a pro, navigating steep dirt paths full of ruts and potholes, ducking under green overhangs, and dodging trash piles and the occasional stray animal. Every few hundred feet, a tree branch would scrape against the windows, and I hoped someone paid for the extra rental insurance.

After ten minutes of bumping along the dirt path, we finally arrived at Tia Ana's home. Jimmy pulled the shuttle over to the side of the path, unable to navigate the muddy driveway that led to a rust-colored cement block structure, seemingly tucked away in the middle of the jungle. As soon as the shuttle stopped, a flood of kids poured out of the building to greet us, followed by a pack of stray dogs weaving between our legs. The children rushed to hug those they recognized from previous visits, while the rest of us got nervous smiles as we tried to high-five everyone.

Inside the house, the atmosphere was worlds apart from anything back in the U.S. While there wasn't much in terms of material wealth, the overwhelming love and sense of community were far more powerful than anything money could buy.

We were given a quick tour of the inside, which mainly consisted of two large open areas with concrete exterior walls, tile floors, and drop ceilings. One area functioned as the kitchen, living room, and dining room. A long makeshift counter separated the cooking space from the dining area, where tables were pushed together to accommodate everyone. A few sofas lined the walls in the living area, and an old TV hung on one wall, its wires and cables tangled and running in all directions. The second open space led to the boys' and girls' bathrooms, several group bedrooms filled with bunk beds, and even doubled as an indoor soccer field.

After the tour, we gathered around Tia Ana, squeezing onto old sofas draped with homemade blankets and afghans, while she shared her harrowing story.

"I left my family when I was just seven years old," she started, speaking through a translator. "I was being abused by my father's siblings and thrown out onto the streets to survive on my own as a prostitute."

We all leaned in, trying to focus on her words, while the sounds of roosters crowing and chickens clucking came from the backyard. Just thirty feet away, the kitchen buzzed with activity as an army of children busily prepared a meal for our large group. We could hear them laughing and singing as they worked together—chopping vegetables, setting plates and silverware, and grilling hot dogs and hamburgers.

Tia Ana continued her story for 45 minutes, and we sat in silence, most of us struggling to hold back tears as she recounted her life on the streets and the hardships she had endured.

Thankfully, decades later, a kind neighbor introduced her to a supportive church community that would dramatically change her life.

"The Lord asked me to start caring for children," Tia Ana continued. "And I told Him, 'I will give up everything, but You must provide for me.'"

With that promise, in 1991, Tia Ana dedicated herself to caring for children who faced hardships similar to her own. Starting with nothing, she lived in a rundown building in a gang-infested slum, caring for over 30 children of local sex workers. In 2019, a group of donors purchased the property where we were now sitting, and Tia Ana moved in that same year to continue her mission of caring for these children.

Her story concluded on a high note as she spoke about Pastor Wally and all those who had supported her family, acknowledging that God had kept His promise. It was evident that she loved these children, and although there had been some rough patches over the years, she was thrilled to see them grow up and succeed in life.

Someone brought out a small speaker, and Katy Perry's music filled the room as we engaged with the children in simple, joyful activities. A group of girls held the speaker over their heads, dancing as if there were no tomorrow. Bags of balloons spilled onto the table, and we all tapped into our balloon animal skills, trying to remember how to make dogs, crowns, and flowers. An impromptu soccer game erupted in the next room, where bedroom doors served as goals. I'm pretty sure at least two ceiling tiles were knocked loose, and I heard at least one light bulb smash. Nobody cared; they were having too much fun.

One boy, Mio, who was about 12 years old, and I connected over magic card tricks despite our language barrier. He performed the same trick repeatedly, each time holding his hands out with a loud "TA-DAH!" while laughing uncontrollably.

He proudly led me to a backyard teeming with chickens, turkeys, and other wildlife, all coexisting beneath a clothesline strung between the trees. He jumped over weathered, completely rusted steps that led to the dirt yard and took my hand to introduce me to "el pavo," the giant turkey that seemed to rule over all the other birds. T-shirts and jeans hung from the clothesline, a sight I hadn't seen since my childhood in the '80s.

Tia Ana moved through the space, checking on lunch and ensuring that everyone felt included, cared for, and at home. Throughout the afternoon, stray dogs wandered in and out, seeking a scratch on their backs or under their chins, or perhaps even a scrap of food. Each dog seemed to have its favorite child, as if they shared a common bond and a silent understanding of what it felt like to be unwanted.

Lunch was served, and it was clear they had this process down to a science. If my wife and I were serving over 30 people, the stress level would be quite high. However, what we witnessed was a well-honed operation, with each child knowing their role in serving or cleanup.

When it was time to start the birthday party, the children's faces lit up as they opened their gifts: toy cars, planes, makeup, lotion, and cheap sunglasses. I've sat in the living room with my own children on Christmas morning, witnessing their mild enthusiasm as they unwrapped gadgets, phones, iPads, sports jerseys, and everything in between. However, these simple items—things we often take for granted—sparked pure joy and gratitude on their faces. There were no electronic gadgets, no phones, and no TV or movies—just a genuine celebration of love.

Philippians 4:13 above the doorway (top), and the group photo at Tia Ana's house

The words "Atodo lo puedo en Cristo que me fortalece," painted above the open doorway in royal blue and framed by colorful flowers, were impossible to miss. This verse from Philippians 4:13 — "I can do all things through Christ who strengthens me"—perfectly captured the spirit of this extraordinary place.

The day concluded with joyful goodbyes, promises to return, and plenty of photos. A few of us stood outside in front of the shuttle, waiting for the others to finish up. As we chatted about the incredible children in the home, Wally was moved to tears. "I've been doing this for years, and this was the best day these kids have ever had."

The evidence of God's work in these kids' lives was everywhere.

CHAPTER 50
IT'S A SCHOOL DAY

Proverbs 22:6 *"Direct your children onto the right path, and when they are older, they will not leave it."*

Tuesday, June 25, 2024. 8:30 AM

Tuesday morning, after another delicious Salvadoran breakfast in the hotel lobby, we piled into the shuttle for a day trip to Cojutepeque. Although the church services had been wonderful so far, today would provide a break from the intense prayer sessions, as we were scheduled to meet with young students at a local school and later with a group of adults eager to learn English. The drive took about an hour, and the atmosphere was relaxed. We spent nearly half the trip engaged in a battle of Dad jokes. I was clearly the winner.

When we arrived at the school, the principal greeted us with a huge smile and thanked us for coming to speak to the students. We quickly learned that many of these kids had faced significant challenges—broken homes, parents in prison, and countless other hardships. We were asked to talk to the students about mental health and resilience, and even offer prayers.

Can you imagine being invited to pray with children at a public school back home? Yeah, that wouldn't fly in the U.S. But here, we had the freedom to dive into sensitive topics. So, earlier in the week when Pastor Stephen asked for volunteers to lead the discussion, I didn't hesitate to jump at the opportunity.

I spent the previous evening preparing notes to ensure I could share relatable stories with the kids. It was challenging, especially since I didn't know their ages, and I had to break everything into bite-sized chunks so the translators could keep the conversation flowing smoothly.

As we got off the bus, we split into three groups, and I was with Hudson, Sid, Kayle, and Brian. The school had an open outdoor layout, with concrete paths dividing the open-air classrooms. These basic setups consisted of classrooms beneath metal roofs, lacking fans or air conditioning, filled with eager young minds sitting in simple metal chairs behind desks that had endured years of use.

Our first classroom of the day was filled with sixth graders. Nothing quiets a room faster than a group of English-speaking gringos walking in on a Tuesday morning. Knowing we couldn't dive right into discussions about feelings, we devised some icebreaker activities to ease the tension. During the bus ride to the school, we all wrote encouraging words on slips of paper and tucked them into balloons. Once we arrived, we began passing out the balloons, and Raul, our translator for the day, explained the game. As soon as I yelled "GO!" the kids were instructed to not let the balloons hit the floor. When I shouted "STOP!" they had to hold onto any balloons they could grab.

"Go!" I yelled, watching a dozen colorful balloons dance in the air.

Whenever I see a balloon aloft, instinct takes over. No matter what else I'm doing, it becomes my sole mission to prevent that balloon from touching the ground. If I were a surgeon, elbow-deep in a patient's guts and connecting a brand-new heart as the transplant neared completion, and a balloon floated across the room, there would be no hesitation. Someone else would have to finish connecting the arteries because that balloon must be saved. For those 10 and 11-year-olds, it was no different.

After about 30 seconds, I shouted, "STOP!" and watched them scramble to secure the nearest balloon.

"If you have a blue balloon, pop it now," I instructed. A little girl with a ponytail, clutching the only blue balloon in the room, looked at me with confusion. "Pop it," I reiterated, mimicking a stabbing motion with my hands. The kids around her began shouting in Spanish, offering her pens and pencils. Finally grasping the idea, she took a pen from a classmate and, after about twelve attempts, the balloon burst. A slip of paper fluttered to her desk with the word "HOPE" scrawled across it.

I handed the slip to Kayle, who shared a few sentences about what that word meant to us and to God. We quickly resumed the game, popping more balloons and sharing the words we discovered. Once I felt we had established rapport, I spoke for a few minutes about who we were, who I was, and some struggles I had faced throughout my life. I aimed to keep the conversation at a sixth-grade level, but discussing feelings of sadness remained a heavy topic.

As I stood there speaking, I couldn't help but notice the teacher sitting in the corner of the room with her eyes closed, looking as if she were asleep. After my initial annoyance, I gradually realized that she had vision problems concealed behind her tinted sunglasses.

I continued for about five minutes, wrapping up by asking them to remember three things:

- It's OK to talk about yourself. Know and recognize when you feel sad and find others you can confide in.
- Seek out other people and help them. "In the U.S.," I told them, "we have a saying: 'How are you?' It doesn't really mean anything; it's just a way of greeting others, like saying '¿Cómo está?'" I explained that the usual response is, "Good, how are you?" I offered different alternatives to genuinely find out how your friend is doing.
- God loves you, and you have a purpose.

As we left the classroom, Raul mentioned we needed to wait for another teacher to escort the blind woman to her next classroom. I felt the Holy Spirit urging me to pray with the woman I hadn't yet spoken to.

"Will you come with me to pray with her?" I asked Raul. We made our way to the corner of the classroom, where she sat in a tiny chair designed for pre-teens. She looked in our direction, and I could see her clouded eyes beneath the sunglasses she wore. Raul asked if we could speak with her for a moment, and she appeared hesitant. Kneeling down, I thanked her for allowing us to spend time in her classroom and told her that God loved her and was proud of all she was doing for the kids.

I felt nervous yet confident. This was the first person I had prayed with who hadn't explicitly asked for it, and I wasn't sure how it would go.

"Is it okay if I pray with you?" I asked, and she nodded her head ever so slightly. I prayed for healing in her eyes and for her vision to return. I then asked her to open her eyes and tell us what she saw. In Spanish, she softly muttered, "No change." After a second prayer, she said it was a little better, though I suspected she was being polite so I would leave her alone. Undeterred, I pressed on, asking, "Can we try one more time?"

"I don't really believe in God; it's probably not going to work," she replied, her eyes cast down at the floor. I felt dejected and glanced over at Raul to gauge his response. He spoke briefly to her in Spanish, then turned to me and said, "It's okay; we tried our best."

It was time to move on to the next classroom, which was filled with ninth graders. We played the same balloon game, and this time it was intense. I liked these kids. Between rounds, I jokingly told them, "If anybody gets hurt, your teacher will be very mad at me!"

I delivered a similar talk about my life experiences, and it felt well received. The usual class clowns in the back whispered to each other and made remarks under their breath. I paced the classroom slowly, standing close to those individuals as I spoke. Throughout my life, I, too, had hidden behind humor rather than facing my emotions. But I was getting to the core of today's topic, hoping to connect with the kids who needed it most.

Knowing that this group was more mature than the previous one, I felt comfortable discussing mental health more directly. I didn't have to rely on phrases like "feeling sad or upset." The room grew quiet when I began talking about suicide and negative thoughts, and I could sense the class clowns hanging on my every word.

After the talk, a few kids approached us to express their gratitude and take pictures. I will probably never know if we truly reached anyone that day, but I believe that because God put us there, there was a purpose in our presence.

As we left the school, I replayed the encounter with the teacher, wondering why our prayers hadn't been answered. I recalled Wally's words about healing and how it's important not to dwell on self-doubt or question why things happen or don't happen. Our goal isn't to win a theological debate; it's simply to pray for someone's healing and give God the glory. I still wonder if our words had any impact on her in the weeks and months that followed. I hope they did.

Our team praying with students in Cojutepeque

CHAPTER 51
LANGUAGE BARRIERS AND BRIDGES

1 Thessalonians 5:11 "*So encourage each other and build each other up, just as you are already doing.*"

Tuesday, June 25, 2024. 2:30 PM

After leaving the school, we took a short ride to a local church in Cojutepeque, where we would spend the afternoon. There, we were set to meet a group of adult English learners, ranging from late teens to middle-aged individuals, all eager—though probably more like compelled—to practice their English-speaking skills with native speakers. Having studied English for about six months, their goal was to engage in natural conversation. While this wasn't explicitly about ministry or faith, we were encouraged to remain open to the Holy Spirit's guidance during our interactions.

The church, Iglesia de Cristo Bajo su Gracia, was situated at the southern end of the city, accessible only by navigating the crowded streets that barely accommodated our shuttle bus. Once again, Jimmy worked his magic, maneuvering us as close to the church as possible before heading off to find a parking spot a few blocks away. Under the sweltering El Salvador sun, we walked up the hill to the church, which featured an open-air section with chairs and an altar, alongside a modest classroom painted a bright lime green. As we entered, we passed by the "bathrooms," which were simply individual toilets behind a wooden door—providing minimal privacy, to say the least.

The atmosphere was relaxed as we enjoyed lunch—ham and cheese sandwiches pulled from the ever-present white cooler that Wally had brought along. Though it was only our fourth day in El Salvador, the experiences had been intense, and I was still mentally processing everything.

Around 1:45 PM, the students began to trickle into the room, creating an atmosphere reminiscent of a middle school dance, with a distinct separation between the boys and girls. Our group settled on one side while the Salvadorans filled the chairs on the opposite side, forming a large circle. As the afternoon was dedicated to speaking only in English, we felt relaxed, although our guests seemed a bit anxious and nervous.

After the English teacher introduced us, we kicked things off with an icebreaker—a giant ball tossed around the room. When someone caught the ball, they would ask a question to the person who threw it. The questions were simple, such as "What's your favorite food?" or "Do you have any pets?" I realized I should incorporate icebreakers into my everyday life because this activity worked like a charm, instantly lightening the mood.

We then split into smaller groups of four—two Salvadorans and two Americans—to encourage more personal conversations. We spent about five minutes tossing questions back and forth before switching groups when the teacher called time. Some discussions flowed effortlessly, while others felt a bit more… well, rudimentary. In one group, there was a young teenage girl dressed entirely in black who appeared incredibly shy and barely engaged. Each time I directed a question her way, she whispered to the person next to her, her hand shielding her face.

Despite the difficulty connecting with her, I felt a deep sense of empathy. As I walked away, I sensed a strong nudge from the Holy Spirit; a vivid image formed in my mind of her standing in a circle of people, confidently speaking English, with God standing right behind her, His hand on her shoulder, beaming with pride. I knew I had to share a word from God with her.

When I glanced back to see which group she was joining next, I caught her looking at me, and I couldn't help but wonder if the Holy Spirit had whispered something to her as well.

The small groups continued, and after approximately 45 minutes of "speed talking," we transitioned to our next set of activities: Taboo, charades, and a session with a small device that emitted electric shocks.

There is an episode of *The Simpsons* titled "There's No Disgrace Like Home," in which Homer uses shock therapy to enhance family communication. Apparently, in real life, a company has created a "shock machine" designed to "improve communication." When the teacher unveiled a small yellow box adorned with Homer and Bart stickers and gave a quick tutorial on how the box worked, we all burst into laughter. Well, the Americans laughed; the students did not. The contraption consisted of a voltage knob and two metal sticks connected by wires, and the game was straightforward: the fewer points you scored, the more likely you were to receive a chance to "improve communications."

I'll admit, the rounds of Taboo and charades were a blast, showcasing how effective communication can transcend language barriers, especially when gestures and expressions come into play. Honestly, the shocks weren't that bad—or at least I wouldn't know because my group emerged victorious.

As the event began to wind down and we started saying our goodbyes, I turned to Sid, one of my teammates who spoke Spanish, and asked, "Can I borrow you for a quick translation?" Together, we approached the girl in black, who appeared visibly uncomfortable. I didn't hesitate; I dove right in. "While we were in the group earlier, I felt that God was prompting me to speak with you."

Her eyes locked onto mine, and I noticed her relax just a bit.

I continued, "He wants you to know that He is so proud of you, especially for stepping out of your comfort zone to learn another language."

Tears welled up in her eyes as she absorbed Sid's translation. I gently placed my hand on her shoulder and said, "Don't feel embarrassed if your English isn't perfect. Keep working hard, and He will reveal many wonderful things in your future."

She wiped away her tears, thanked me, and turned to rejoin her friends waiting nearby. If I had confirmed something she had been thinking or praying about, then that was good enough for me. I loved how God was using me to speak to others.

The Simpson's Shocker in action

CHAPTER 52
BUILDING MORE BRIDGES

John 14:16–18 *"And I will ask the Father, and he will give you another Advocate, who will never leave you."*

Wednesday, June 26, 2024. 5:00 PM

The following day, we had another opportunity to engage with adults studying English, similar to our previous session in Cojutepeque. This time, it was a quick jaunt across town to a small mission church where we would interact with students ranging from their late teens to mid-40s. We hopped off the shuttle, waved goodbye to Jimmy, and walked into an open-air classroom where the teacher greeted us with a warm smile. She explained the plan in English: we would break into small groups and practice by asking each other questions.

She dismissed the class, instructing her students to introduce themselves to us so we could form small groups.

I scanned the room and noticed a group of three, so I approached them and invited one of the young women outside for a one-on-one conversation. Her English was impressive, as if she had been studying for years. Our discussion flowed smoothly as we talked about everything from family to favorite foods and movies. When I asked about her career goals, she shared her ambition to work in a call center—a burgeoning industry in El Salvador that offers salaries significantly above minimum wage, making it a highly desirable career path.

After about ten minutes, the teacher called for everyone to switch groups, so we wrapped up our conversation. I looked around and noticed a woman in her mid-30s sitting on a bench with a smile, patiently waiting for the next person to join her. I walked over, returned her smile, and said, "Hi, my name is Ben. What's your name?"

Her smile widened, and in flawless English, she replied, "Hi! How are you? I'm Luz; it's great to meet you!"

The conversation flowed effortlessly as we discussed our backgrounds and families. This was a refreshing change from yesterday's Q&A sessions, which primarily revolved around questions like "What's your favorite food?" or "Do you like movies?" I learned that Luz was a psychology teacher and a mother of two, brimming with life and energy. She mentioned that she started studying English to help her children with their schoolwork.

As our conversation went on, I felt a familiar nudge from the Holy Spirit. Another image emerged in my mind; this time, it was God surrounding her as she read to her children from an English book, then taking their hands and guiding them toward a place filled with vibrant colors.

I had a strong sense of what it meant, so I waited for her to finish her thought before asking, "Do you belong to a church?"

When she replied, "No, it's been a long time since I've attended church," I sensed it was an opportunity.

"Can I share something that God placed on my heart for you?" Her features softened immediately, and anticipation was clear in her eyes.

"Yes, of course," she replied eagerly.

"I believe God wants you to know how proud He is of you and that He loves you. You're setting a wonderful example by taking English classes and being a great mother. He sees you, and He is preparing you and your family for amazing things ahead."

Tears welled up in her eyes as she removed her glasses to wipe them. After a few moments, she looked at me and said, "This morning on the drive here, I was praying about this, wondering if I was on the right path...I guess I am."

Chills ran down my spine as the simple message that God loves you and He is proud of you once again provided exactly the encouragement she needed. That was all the confirmation I needed from Him. Once more, I had the privilege of being a vessel for God's affirmation —and it was amazing!

Me and Luz after our English session

CHAPTER 53
MIRACLES IN COMASAGUA

Psalm 34:17 *"The LORD hears his people when they call to him for help. He rescues them from all their troubles."*

Wednesday, June 26, 2024. 5:00 PM

ater that night, we were scheduled to participate in another church service, this time in Comasagua, home to Pastor Jose Luis. Comasagua is a small municipality nestled in the mountains about 45 minutes west of San Salvador. Heavy traffic and stray dogs scattered along the roads transformed our 45-minute drive into a 90-minute trek, leaving me nostalgic for the familiar "traffic" back in North Texas.

As we pulled into the dirt parking lot leading to the church, my gaze was drawn to the cemetery across the street. The sun began to dip behind the lush green mountains, casting eerie shadows across the gravesites. Unlike anything I had seen in the U.S., the cemetery featured individual graves surrounded by simple wooden or metal mini fences, offering a sense of protection for those who had passed. It was a moving blend of mourning and celebration of life.

We exited the shuttle and descended a steep set of steps carved into the hillside, leading us to the buildings that housed both the church and

Pastor Jose Luis's living quarters. He welcomed us with a smile that radiated genuine kindness, and despite the language barrier, his warmth was unmistakable. With little time before the service, we settled into brightly colored sofas and folding chairs as he dove straight into the story of how he became a pastor.

Through Marielos, who was translating that night, Pastor Jose Luis shared how his troubled childhood led him to ministry. His passion for the gospel was ignited not from deep-seated faith but from the promise of getting candy at church. At just 15, he enrolled in a Bible institute and was sent to Guazapa—an area notorious for guerrilla activity during the 1980s—to pastor a small community of about 25 homes. "If you can open a church in three months, you have a calling to ministry; if not, you don't," he was told. Despite the gunfire and chaos, he quickly expanded his ministry, eventually founding not just one but three churches.

As the years passed, he continued to minister in the capital, and his family grew after marrying and welcoming four children. However, his journey was fraught with struggles, including financial hardships and doubts about his calling. "Here in El Salvador, they don't pay pastors, and we had four children. Sometimes, we went weeks without eating. Yet, every time, God provided."

One Christmas Eve, feeling the weight of his family's hunger, Pastor Jose Luis prayed to God for help. "Soon after, there was a knock at my door," he recalled. A man stood there and said, "It's Christmas, and people are usually busy cooking. I don't see any activity in your kitchen, so I thought I would bring you some food." The man left a few days' worth of provisions and quietly departed. "A few minutes later, my kids complained about being thirsty, and before they could even finish their words, the unknown man returned and said, 'Sorry, I forgot the drinks.'"

Years later, Pastor Jose Luis's wife received a revelation from God about a small town where young people were struggling. A few days after the revelation, he was invited to preach in that town, and when they arrived, she said, "This is the town that God showed me, and He is going to bring us here."

I didn't know where he was taking the story, but I found myself glued to my seat in eager anticipation.

"Over the years, different groups offered assistance, but we still didn't have enough," he said. One day, he finally broke. "I began to tell God, 'For 19 years, I have served, and You have never given me what I need- ed,'" Pastor Jose Luis said. "'If You're going to kill me, kill me now. You told me You would provide for me, but You're not. So, I am done being a pastor.'"

When he went inside to tell his wife, she informed him that a man from the U.S. had called to set up a meeting for the next day. "I don't care," he told her. "I'm not changing my mind." Pastor Jose Luis candidly admitted, "Forgive me for what I'm about to say, but I was tired of Americans who came, took pictures of us, offered us things, and then left, never to be seen or heard from again."

"The next day, I answered the knock at the door and found Pastor Wally standing there." He paused, looking down at the floor and rubbing his eyes. As had become customary that week, we all sat in silence, not wanting to breathe too hard for fear of missing a single word. I couldn't help but join him in tears.

"Wally spoke the exact words that changed everything: 'God heard what you said yesterday, and I was sent to take care of you.'"

"I had never received a hug from a pastor," he said, his voice choked with emotion. "That was 15 years ago."

He recalled how everything changed for his family the day Wally entered their lives. When Wally first saw their inadequate living condi- tions—lacking sanitation services—he encouraged them, saying, "Get a better house." When Pastor Jose Luis voiced his financial concerns, Wally reassured him, "That's not your problem; that's my problem."

With God's guidance and Wally's support, they secured a new home for $500, which felt overwhelming at the time. Eventually, they moved to Comasagua, the town that God had revealed to his wife. In their new community, the rent dropped to just $25 a month, allowing them to use the remaining funds to provide meals three times a week for over 100 hungry children.

As he spoke, you could hear the pride in his voice when he talked about how his four children thrived against the odds, supported by families like Wally's who encouraged their educational dreams—something so rare among pastors' children in El Salvador. He proudly shared how each child had achieved their goals: his oldest had graduated, one son was attending university, another trained as a chef, and the youngest was pursuing nursing.

Now, as we prepared to walk over to the church for service, Pastor Jose Luis concluded his testimony, saying, "Our dream is that from here, God's anointing flows everywhere. Thank you, God bless you, and now, it's time to go to church!"

Pastor Jose Luis shares his testimony

The atmosphere in the room was thick with emotion and anticipation, reminding me of countless locker room pep talks minutes before a big game. The church worship team was already playing next door, and their music drifted down the hill into Pastor Jose Luis's living room, warming up the crowd like a marching band before the team comes out onto the field.

As we walked back up the steps toward the church, not a word was spoken. We entered a structure unlike any church I had known in the U.S. It resembled a barn, with corrugated metal walls and a roof, a concrete floor, and concrete steps that served as stadium seating. The stage was dressed in black paint, and the sound and lighting were perfect.

We filled the first row of tan plastic lawn chairs as we listened to the worship team energize the crowd. Little kids danced, older women raised their hands to the sky, and people swayed back and forth, singing and clapping along. After a couple of songs, our City Point worship team was called up to the stage to continue playing. I say this with the utmost respect for the church's worship team because they were great, but it felt like we were at a concert where the opening act had just given way to the headliner.

The music was so powerful, and the congregation was fully engaged, the power of God evident. Even Jimmy, our trusty driver, was jumping around and hugging everyone, completely immersed in the worship experience.

I stood on one of the concrete steps toward the back of the church, soaking everything in. Pastor Julie led the band as they launched into a song called *"Yeshua,"* sung entirely in Spanish. It didn't matter; we didn't need an interpreter to know that God was present in the room.

The rhythmic melodies filled the air, accompanied by guitar and drums.

"Yeshuuuuu uu ah...aaaaah aaah aaaaah, aaaah AAAAh aaaaah."

The instruments quieted down, leaving just the keyboard.

"Yeshuuuuu uu ah...aaaaah aaah aaaaah, aaaah AAAAh aaaaah."

It continued for at least ten minutes, yet time stood still. The music had long faded away, leaving only voices to fill the barn that served as God's house. Hands were raised all around. I watched tears roll down the faces of those nearby. I heard the sound of foreign tongues spread throughout the congregation.

"*Yeshuuuuu uu ah…aaaaah aaah aaaaah, aaaah AAAAh aaaaah.*"

Pastor Wally, scheduled to deliver the sermon that night, read the room perfectly and skipped right over the message so we could go into ministry for the people.

Pastor Julie stood on the stage, gripping the mic with purpose, her voice carrying the kind of conviction that made you wanna get up out of your chair. It wasn't loud, but it was powerful—motivational, direct, and filled with the energy of someone preaching with their whole heart:

> **"If you need prayer, if you need healing, if you need a miracle—whatever you need, the Holy Spirit has filled this place. God is here for you tonight."**

Her words seemed to reach into the very soul of the room, leaving no doubt that they were spoken with divine certainty.

I joined Raul and Chris at the front of the stage, flanked on our left and right by other team members. Before the translator could finish the last of Pastor Julie's words, a line of individuals began to form.

A frail older woman slowly hobbled up to us. It was evident that she was in pain before she even opened her mouth to speak.

"What's your name?" I asked, raising my voice to be heard over the music.

"Rosario," she replied, looking at Raul for translation.

"What can we pray for with you?"

As soon as she began speaking to Raul, I felt the Holy Spirit give me words to share with the woman in front of us. This time, it was more of a feeling than a picture, but as the words formed in my mind, they were accompanied by the warm squeeze of God's confirmation, assuring me that I had heard it correctly.

Raul informed us that she was suffering from severe back pain and persistent throat pain that had lasted for years.

Was this me again? How many people would I see this week with back pain and thyroid problems?!

"Rosario," I said, placing my hand on her shoulder and looking her in the eyes. "I believe God has something to share with you tonight. Your life has been filled with many wonderful things, but He still has so much more for you to accomplish. He knows how much you love your children and all your grandchildren. You need not worry, for they will all find God."

She looked at me for a moment, stunned, and then said, "I have 10 grandchildren, and I've been worried that not all of them have accepted Jesus."

"He knows," I replied. "And it's OK." I began to pray, commanding healing over her back and throat. "How do you feel? The same, better, or worse?"

"It's a little better," she said.

"Okay, can we pray again?" She nodded, and I continued, "How do you feel now?" I asked after the second prayer.

Rosario looked at the three of us, reached up to rub her neck, and then bent over slightly as if she were going to touch her toes. "I feel good," she said, a bit tentatively.

"No more pain?" Raul asked.

"No, none," she replied, wiping tears away from her eyes. We spent a few more minutes talking, and she thanked us before returning to her seat.

We had just witnessed yet another miracle from God.

Others came forward that night for prayer, including a young teenage girl suffering from depression and a family seeking prayer for their new baby.

Toward the end of the night, another older woman slowly approached us. "What's your name?" Raul asked.

"Gabriela," she replied.

"What can we pray for tonight?" Raul asked.

She explained that she needed shoulder surgery and that the pain was quite severe. "How bad?" I asked. "On a scale of 1 to 10?"

"An 11," she replied, clearly not understanding how the 1 to 10 scale works. She attempted to lift her left arm to demonstrate, barely managing to move it away from her side.

She continued, telling Raul, "And my knee. I can't walk up and down stairs without pain."

Instantly, I recalled Sunday afternoon at Pastor Wally's house and heard a joking voice in my head, complete with a full Rodney Danger-field accent: *"I can do shoulders. I can do knees. That's easy!"* I was quite sure it was the Holy Spirit fulfilling Pastor Wally's words that Jesus was going to mess with me that week.

I couldn't help but laugh out loud. As she stared at me like I was a crazy person, I explained the dialogue that had just occurred inside my head. It didn't translate well, and she continued to stare, clearly thinking I was a crazy American. Maybe Rodney Dangerfield wasn't well-known in the hills of El Salvador.

I gently placed my hand on her shoulder and prayed. When I finished, she lifted her arm nearly parallel to the floor, her expression shifting as if she was beginning to believe something was happening. After the second prayer, she said her pain had dropped to a two and raised her arm even higher.

"Let's do it one more time," I said, continuing with the same prayer.

"Okay, Gabriela, how does it feel now?" She opened her eyes, trying to contain her excitement as both arms lifted straight up into the air, pain-free. I was filled with absolute joy and couldn't contain my laughter.

"You know what this means now, right?" I asked her. "Now you worship with both hands raised instead of just one."

She chuckled, as Chris took over and prayed over her knee. Kneeling down, I placed one hand on her knee and felt her start shaking and crying, so we quickly got a chair behind her to prevent her from falling. The prayer continued for a while, and in the end, we watched God heal her completely, leaving her pain-free.

After we finished, I was talking to Raul when Chris turned to us and said, "Look at that." We followed his gaze and watched her bound up the concrete steps as she exited the back of the church.

As the lines thinned and the prayer team wrapped up, Pastor Jose Luis shared some final words with the congregation before dismissing them. We observed as the congregation slowly made their way out of the church, clapping each other on the back and engaging in lively conversation. Our team gathered at the front of the stage to huddle around Pastor Jose Luis, listening as Lyric, one of our team members, shared a word with him.

"God showed me a vision of many children filling the church, singing and sitting on each other's laps," Lyric said, Pastor Jose Luis listening intently to every translated word. "This was the place to be on a Wednesday night."

Through tears, Pastor Jose Luis shared that they had recently created a special space for kids, but there were complaints that they wanted to be IN the service instead of being stuck outside.

"I have been praying about it, and this is confirmation from God that we need to make a change. Thank you," Pastor Jose Luis said.

Sitting quietly on the shuttle back to the hotel that night, I felt an overwhelming sense of gratitude—not just for the miracles we'd witnessed, but for the bond we shared in that simple space. Every story, every prayer, and every step of faith felt like threads coming together to form something bigger. Though we came from different places and backgrounds, it was clear: we were all part of something far greater than ourselves.

Praying and worshiping in Comasagua

CHAPTER 54
THE VOLCANO

Matthew 6:26 *"Look at the birds. They don't plant or harvest or store food in barns, for your heavenly Father feeds them. And aren't you far more valuable to him than they are?"*

Thursday, June 27, 2024. 9:00 AM

The next morning, we enjoyed a leisurely hotel breakfast of scrambled eggs, cheese, fried plantains, mashed beans, and rich coffee (yes, the same as before, and yes, still delicious). Afterward, we loaded the van for a morning adventure at Parque Nacional El Boquerón, where the San Salvador volcano towers over 6,000 feet above sea level within the national park.

Once Jimmy skillfully maneuvered the shuttle into a parking spot, we piled out and headed to the trailhead for a pleasant 20-minute climb to the volcano's rim. Like much of the city, stray dogs were everywhere— friendly, not aggressive, just hoping for a head pat and perhaps some food. As we gathered at the trailhead for a group picture, a light brown dog with a black muzzle immediately took a liking to us.

For some reason, this dog joined our group with a sense of purpose, and I immediately dubbed him Mike, the Dog. When we paused for a group photo, Mike waited patiently while we lined up and smiled for the camera. As we ascended the trail, Mike led the way, frequently glancing back to ensure we were still close behind. Whenever someone stopped to rest, Mike patiently waited until the entire group was ready to move again.

Mike guided us to the summit, where we were greeted by stunning views of the lush green caldera below. It felt like he instinctively knew we had arrived. At the top stood an observation tower—a striking two-story metal-and-glass structure offering breathtaking views of the volcano. While we climbed the steps to take it all in, Mike rested on a concrete bench, seemingly unimpressed, as if he had seen it all before.

At the second story, those unafraid of heights stepped onto the glass platform, peering straight down into the dizzying drop below. I walked to the platform's edge, leaning against the rail and soaking in the view. As I stood in silence, gazing at God's natural wonders, I reflected on everything I had witnessed that week. In that moment, I felt truly alive—an integral part of His plan, just like everyone else around me.

Time seemed to stand still as I watched massive black birds glide effortlessly across the crater, never once flapping their wings as they rode the air currents. They appeared to not have a single care in the world. As I observed them float in wide arcs across the volcano, I could sense how easy it was to let my worries melt away.

After a few minutes of reflection and, of course, countless photos, we made our way back down from the platform to the top of the trail. I looked around, hoping to find Mike the Dog waiting to guide us back down, but he was nowhere to be seen.

As we began our leisurely descent, I couldn't shake thoughts of the brown mutt, even after having seen hundreds that morning alone. God provides for us in countless ways, even through what might seem like a trivial gesture—like having Mike guide a group of gringos to the top of a volcano. I thought about how often I had felt alone in my life, never fully realizing that I was not truly alone at all. He had always been with me, sending someone or something to guide me, to offer encouragement, and to fulfill whatever role He had for them.

Today was no different. Mike had played his part, and now it was time for him to move on to the next role that God had for him. And tonight, God was preparing me to play another part in a story I could never have imagined.

Mike the dog resting on the trail.

CHAPTER 55
SPIRITUAL WARFARE IN SAN MARTIN

Ephesians 6:10 "*Therefore, put on every piece of God's armor so you will be able to resist the enemy in the time of evil. Then after the battle you will still be standing firm.*"

Thursday, June 27, 2024. 7:15 PM

There's a scene in *The Truman Show*, a Jim Carrey movie from 1998, where Truman attempts to escape town, only to find that every road out is mysteriously obstructed. Traffic jams appear out of nowhere, detours force him in circles, and no matter which way he turns, something blocks his path. Someone is working behind the scenes to keep him from uncovering the truth.

In movies, we call it art. In life, we might call this spiritual warfare.

This was our reality as we attempted to reach an evening service in San Martin. We were already about 15 minutes behind schedule when a few people in our group realized they had forgotten some items in their hotel room. Traffic was typically bad during rush hour, but tonight was an absolute nightmare. Jimmy, leading the charge from the driver's seat, did his best to find shortcuts, but there was no quick way to reach our destination. Every street he turned onto was instantly filled with cars, trucks, and buses that seemed to have appeared out of thin air.

Cell phone coverage was spotty at best during the drive, leaving us unable to call Wally to inform him we were running late. Jimmy's phone rang a couple of times, displaying Wally's name on the caller ID, but the signal was too weak for him to answer.

I didn't fully realize it at that moment, but something dark knew we were coming and didn't want us there.

We passed through some of the most impoverished villages I had ever seen. Makeshift structures, constructed from wooden poles and rusted metal roofs, lined the uneven and cracked pavement, which eventually gave way to dirt paths. A village typically consisted of a few simple structures made from corrugated metal sheets and wood. Everywhere we looked, the lack of resources, proper infrastructure, and even basic amenities was painfully evident.

Throughout the drive, wild dogs sought refuge along the roads in search of food. Often, they wouldn't even budge or glance in our direction; it was up to Jimmy to maneuver around them.

Two hours and fifteen minutes later, we arrived at the church. Music pulsed from the open windows and the place was filled with a much younger crowd that night. We wove our way through the congregation to find seats among a sea of green plastic lawn chairs. It felt more like an automotive garage than a church, and there was even an old car parked in the back corner of the building. A large black banner hung proudly on the wall behind the worship team, emblazoned with the word "Jesus" in bold white letters.

The air buzzed with energy, and the thunderous rain pounding against the metal roof only heightened the crowd's excitement. As I stood there, I prayed, asking whether there was anyone I could help that night. I immediately envisioned a man wearing a white shirt with black writing, a hat, and glasses. He was on a boat in a vast body of water, surrounded by storms. The boat rocked, and he appeared fearful, symbolizing the struggle he was facing. Then, in this vision, Jesus appeared, calmed the storm, and guided the boat safely to its destination.

When I opened my eyes, I glanced to my left and saw a man leaning against the wall. He wore a black shirt with white writing. *"That's not him,"* I muttered to myself as I continued scanning the room. Doubt began to creep in; maybe I had the junior varsity version of this whole prophetic word thing. I looked back, and one of the translators, David, had his hand on the man's shoulder as he prayed for him. *"Okay, maybe this IS the guy."*

The music blared through the speakers as I walked over to David and waited for him to finish. When he stopped praying with the man, I shouted into his ear, "Hey, I just saw this image..." I relayed what I had seen and stood there for a few minutes, waiting to hear what he would say or if he needed anything else from me. David nodded, yelled "Thanks!" and then went back to listening to the music. At that moment, I wondered if I had the wrong guy. Or maybe my American English didn't translate well to David. Perhaps there was something else happening that I didn't know about. Or maybe I should just keep my junior varsity words to myself.

Worship underway in San Martin

I quickly put it out of my mind as we were called to the front for prayer. That night, I was once again paired with Raul and, for the first time that week, Hudson.

The first person to approach us was a teenage boy who said his back had been bothering him. In the best possible way, this was beginning to sound routine. I smiled upon hearing his ailment, knowing that God had presented a familiar issue and wanted the boy to be healed. We prayed, and the teenager walked away beaming after the pain vanished.

Next was a family: a husband, wife, and their young son, maybe around 10 years old. The wife asked us to pray for their marriage, and I immediately sensed they were dealing with trauma. I saw an image of the three of them in a tight embrace, surrounded by white light, with God's face shining down on them. It seemed they had experienced some kind of loss, though I wasn't certain what it was.

"God is showing me that He loves each of you and understands your pain," I said. "He wants you to continue the love you share for one another, especially for your son, and He will bless you." Raul added a few words, and I watched the family draw even closer as he spoke. Tears streamed down the husband and wife's faces, and when he finished, they thanked us and embraced in a big group hug.

Another teenager approached after the family left. With a teenage, smart-aleck grin that I've seen countless times in my own house, he asked if God had a prophetic word for him. In my head, I asked the Holy Spirit if there was anything that this boy needed to hear, and I immediately envisioned the scene from Tuesday morning in the 9th-grade class in Cojutepeque, with the class clowns huddled in the back. I knew without a doubt what it meant.

Suddenly, a commotion erupted to our left, but I ignored it and focused on the young man in front of me. I asked if he received bad grades, and he replied, "Yes, sometimes."

"The Lord sees you and knows you're a bit of a jokester," I began. "He wants you to know you should balance your sense of humor with a greater seriousness in your studies."

This likely wasn't the prophetic word he had hoped for when he gathered the courage to come forward. His face flushed slightly, and he looked down at his shoes sheepishly. Raul and I continued, and we spent a few minutes telling him that God loved him, and he would become a great leader if he worked hard to get there. He thanked us, and a genuine smile finally broke across his face as he walked away.

As soon as we finished, I turned to see what was happening beside us. A man, perhaps in his late 30s, dressed in a black golf shirt and hat, was struggling physically, as if engaged in a wrestling match with an invisible opponent. Two men from the church had their hands on him, guiding him from the side toward the front. Raul approached, and I eagerly followed to see what was happening.

Raul spoke to the man for a few moments before turning to me and saying, "He has something inside him; let's pray for him."

What? Holy. Crap.[1]

CHAPTER 56
THE MAN IN THE MIRROR

Ephesians 2:10 *"For we are God's masterpiece. He has created us anew in Christ Jesus, so we can do the good things he planned for us long ago."*

Thursday, June 27, 2024. 8:45 PM

I felt as if I were watching this man on my television at home. As if the camera shots were taken by a drone, starting with a tight close-up of the actor while the drone slowly climbed away from the building and panned out to cover the entire country of El Salvador.

My mind wandered for a few seconds, contemplating what exactly I could do next. *I am not at all prepared for this.*

But I was prepared. At that exact moment, in this building full of believers in San Martin, El Salvador, a realization smacked me in the face: every day this week, one by one, God had placed someone in front of me who was a mirror image of myself, desperately seeking prayer. I don't mean they resembled me physically, and they certainly weren't choosing me at the altar because I was the best-looking guy in the group. God was leading them to me, just as He had led me to City Point. And once they stood before me, He held up a full-length mirror, revealing the broken man who had stood before Him last September.

Three days ago, when Maria approached me in Quezaltepeque, I could physically feel the pain in her joints and understood the difficulty she had swallowing due to her thyroid issues because I had been there. In Comasagua, when Gabriela told me her shoulder was an 11 out of 10 on the pain scale and that pain in her right knee prevented her from walking up and down stairs, I knew exactly where she was coming from.

And the man with diabetes and vision problems, battling severe depression and riddled with thoughts of suicide while doubting whether God existed at all...? That was me. Though I could physically see with my own eyes, I was spiritually blinded by something evil, something dark.

Whatever emotional challenges they faced. Whatever spiritual abyss they found themselves in. Whatever ailment, ache, pain, or longing to hear God's voice. They were me.

Less than a year ago, I had been the one knocking at the door of City Point Church—not because I believed God could heal me, but because I was desperate for help. By asking for help, I gained spiritual sight. I overcame my anxiety and suicidal ideations. I battled my own demons, and with God, I triumphed.

But salvation didn't mean the battles were over. One night, months after I was saved, I woke to something I can only describe as other-worldly.

It was sometime around 4:00 AM, and I was dead asleep when some-thing grabbed my ankle and pulled me toward the end of the bed—hard. It wasn't subtle or imagined—it was forceful and undeniable. I shot up, heart pounding, and turned on the lights. My first instinct was to search the room, expecting to find some logical explanation, but there was nothing there. I looked at my ankle for marks or signs. Noth-ing. My dogs were looking at me with curiosity. Eleanor was still asleep.

The fear was real, but it didn't paralyze me. I knew what I had to do. Grabbing my Bible, I went outside and sat under the stars, praying for

God's protection. As I prayed, I felt the fear dissipate, replaced by a calm that only He could provide.

That night reminded me of a simple truth: spiritual battles don't stop when you come to Christ—they often intensify. But I also learned that His power is far greater than any darkness. Now, armed with the confidence of His power and healing, I was ready to help someone battle their own demons.

I felt the drone swoop down again, and the camera quickly zoomed in as a small group of us gathered around the man who was now physically fighting off whatever was inside him.

I placed my hand on the man's back; he was a hot, sweaty mess. He grunted, making sounds like he was in labor as he crossed his arms and gripped his shirt tightly.

Whispers of prayer swirled around the man as the music played in the background.

"In the name of Jesus..."

There were moments when he nearly collapsed, barely held up by the hands reaching in to pray for him.

"All contracts are broken... in the name of Jesus..."

One of the locals gently grasped the man, placing his hands around the back of his head to speak directly into his ear.

"I command you to leave this man..."

"¿Cómo te llamas?" I heard Raul ask the man gently.

There was no response. The man in black continued to grip his shirt, pulling harder.

"No weapons formed against him..."

"¿Cómo te llamas?" Raul asked again, this time more firmly.

The response finally came. Though I couldn't make out the words, it sounded like an angry grunt.

As he swayed back and forth, more and more of us gathered around him to pray. The cycle continued for another 20 minutes before the man finally calmed down. After the storm subsided, we sat him in a plastic lawn chair while two men from the church continued praying with him. I had been so focused on what was right in front of me that I didn't notice most of the congregation had already left and that the house lights were on.

The last hour had been so intense; my shirt was drenched, and I was exhausted and exhilarated all at the same time.

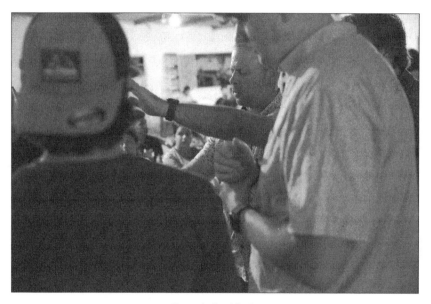

Prayer in San Martin

CHAPTER 57
BUT IS HE HEALED?

Psalm 107:28-29 *"'Lord, help!' they cried in their trouble, and he saved them from their distress. He calmed the storm to a whisper and stilled the waves."*

Thursday, June 27, 2024. 9:45 PM

I f this were a novel or a Hollywood film, this chapter would end in dramatic fashion. As the director called out "ACTION!" I would take the cross from my jacket pocket and boldly shove it into the man's face. The demon would leap from his mouth, scurry across the concrete floor, and take one last evil look back over its shoulder before pointing an outstretched talon at me and running off into the night.

That would have been awesome.

But that didn't happen. However, before we loaded the shuttle to return to our hotel, what did happen was even more amazing.

About five minutes later, our team slowly migrated to the side of the church to recount our experiences.

Raul walked over to the group and said, "The guy feels a lot better now." I looked over and saw him sitting in the chair, staring wordlessly at his shoes.

"Hey, what was that guy's name, anyway?" I asked Raul.

"I don't know; I never got it," he replied.

"Wait, didn't you ask him? I heard him grunt something."

"Oh, no. That was one of the demons I was speaking to."

Say what now? Pretty sure my jaw dropped all the way to the concrete floor.

"So," Raul continued, "I was trying to get the thing inside him to speak to me. The demon said *'We are many,'* and then something that sounded Greek—but I didn't understand exactly what it was."

Of course. Why wouldn't he be talking directly to the demon? Or multiple demons. In Greek.

Suddenly, another commotion broke out, and a chair was kicked over. I looked back and saw the man in the black shirt trying to escape. He took a few drunken swings at the men helping him, and eventually, they bear-hugged him in the corner of the church, behind the old car parked in the back.

Well, I guess that was a failure. It felt like this was the final exam, and though I went down swinging, I had failed the course spectacularly.

Raul turned back to us and, as if he were reading my thoughts, said, "It's okay, we did what we could for him. I think there is a darker family curse that is present, and I'm not sure that the man was ready to surrender to God yet. And, you should know that demons only manifest themselves when they feel threatened. We don't want the demon to manifest violently because that would embarrass the man. So, we did our jobs tonight, and that's a good sign. You all did great."

As we continued discussing the experience, David walked up and stood next to me.

"Hey, David!" I greeted him. "Did you get a chance to tell that guy about the boat in the storm?" It had been hours since I saw the image of the man in the white shirt struggling to maintain his balance in the rocking boat.

"Yes, I told him," said David matter-of-factly.

"Oh? Was it after I walked away? Because I didn't see you talking to him again."

"No," he replied. "I told him about five minutes before you walked over."

For the second time in just a few minutes, I wore a confused dog look, my head cocked to the side. "What do you mean?"

"Before you came over, I saw the same thing you did. There was a guy in a white shirt with black writing, wearing a hat and glasses. I saw him standing on a boat in a big body of water, surrounded by storms. The boat was rocking, and he was afraid until Jesus appeared to him, calmed the storm, and then led him to his destination. That's why I went over to pray with him, to tell him that whatever he was going through, the Lord was with him and would help him through it. I felt it was the correct word from the Holy Spirit because he started crying right away."

Amid a mix of laughter, shock, surprise, and tears, I realized that this wasn't the final exam. It was a small quiz, a brief assignment from the Lord to check my faith. For the past week, every morning when I woke up to the light of day, little seeds of doubt would be planted in my mind.

Did I really pray for that person and then have Jesus heal them? Maybe she didn't understand the pain scale. Maybe her mind tricked her into thinking that my prayer helped take the pain away.

But now, hearing what David just said, it all clicked.

God was right here, at this moment, in this very church.

He was with me all week.

He's been with me this whole year.

He's always been with me, even though I didn't realize it.

He was the light shining through the dark clouds that surrounded me, even when I wasn't looking in His direction.

He saw me before I was born. Every day of my life was recorded in His book. Every moment was laid out before a single day had passed.

He has had this story in mind since the dawn of creation, and I have been walking through the pages of His book my entire life.

This has been His story all along. And I'm finally listening.

From left to right - Raul, me, David, and Lyric

CHAPTER 58
GOD HAS ORDERED MY STEPS

Psalm 139:16 "*You saw me before I was born. Every day of my life was recorded in your book. Every moment was laid out before a single day had passed.*"

Saturday, June 29, 2024. 2:37 PM

We had just boarded the flight back to Dallas, and I found myself with a few quiet hours to reflect on the week. In eight days, I experienced spiritual growth that I could never have comprehended at any other time in my life. It was as if God had been waiting for this precise moment to unlock something within me.

As others plugged headphones into their ears, staring at their phones while watching movies or playing games, I gazed out the window at the landscape below. In my mind, I began to see how events, conversations, and people I had encountered throughout my life were all falling into place—like I had a bird's-eye view of an escape room, with the manual in hand showing how the puzzles were crafted. Not only had God perfectly ordered my steps, but He had also intricately arranged the steps of everyone else, intertwining our lives at just the right moments.

Throughout my life, I've cheated death more times than I can count. There were moments in the cockpit that left me certain it was the end, times on the flight deck where disaster was seconds away, and more close calls behind the wheel of a car than I care to admit.

Each time, I walked away, surprised and grateful to be alive. But back then, I never stopped to acknowledge the One who had protected me. I didn't turn to God and say, "Thank you."

Looking back now, I can see His hand in all those moments. It wasn't luck or instinct—it was His grace. He wasn't done with me yet. Every one of those experiences was preparing me for what was to come, for the person He was shaping me to be:

- Every hour spent in the wrestling room.
- The Ouija board with Jake.
- Going with my mom to hear about the Naval Academy.
- The path to aviation and becoming an NFO.
- Getting E-2Cs instead of jets.
- Meeting Eleanor at a Taco Bell in the food court.
- Always getting my second choice of assignments.
- The Camarillo house.
- Finding the preschool that led to the Christmas Eve service in the barn.
- Choosing retirement over a prestigious career opportunity in the Navy.
- Moving to Texas.
- The meltdown at my brother's wedding.
- The Texas house, meeting Gina, and hearing from Pappy
- Travis getting invited to a Wednesday night Youth Group
- Pastor Stephen answering the door at 9:00 AM.

And finally, this trip to El Salvador, where I witnessed firsthand the power of God, Jesus, and the Holy Spirit in ways I could never have imagined.

I reflected on the start of the week when Marielos pulled me aside on Sunday and said, "God wants you to know that you are going to be a cornerstone and change someone's life. Even if what you have to say is embarrassing, it's okay to share it."

Those words were exactly what I needed to hear; they prepared me to be vulnerable and share my story with the team, students, and those seeking prayer.

Then there was Mike the Dog, faithfully guiding us up the volcano peak—like God leading us through the unfamiliar, revealing the wonders of His creation along the way. It was yet another reminder that God's plan is always at work, even when we don't fully understand it, and that He places the right people (or in this case, animals) in our lives to help us along the journey.

Later in the week, after our last service in San Martin, I sat next to Marielos on the ride home. It was late, and we had all had a long day. We talked about everything we had witnessed. She and the other translators weren't just language converters—they were students of God, in tune with the Holy Spirit. For every miracle I witnessed that week, they had seen hundreds, perhaps even thousands. Despite our differing backgrounds, I learned so much from being around them.

Forty-five minutes into the ride, she looked me in the eyes and asked, "What are you thinking?" I had just finished recounting my experience with the man possessed by a demon. "I don't know… this is all crazy," I muttered, still processing everything. She didn't blink as she said, "The Holy Spirit is telling me that you are ashamed, and you shouldn't be." She never took her eyes off mine, as if she had a direct line to my soul.

I held her gaze for a few seconds, unsure of how to respond. I felt shame, but I didn't know why. She was right—or, I should say, God was right. Perhaps it was because I couldn't heal the man or drive out his demons, which felt like the ultimate test of this trip. Or maybe it was because I had battled my own demons, and being confronted with everything again reopened old wounds. I rested my head against the window, contemplating her words on the rest of the ride back to the hotel.

Now, as our plane began its descent into Dallas, the familiar skyline came into view through my tiny airplane window, and in that moment, God's soft, gentle whisper to me nine months ago was no longer a mystery.

"You Need to Tell Your Story."

I hadn't fully understood those words until now. I thought I was close a few times, and I'd had some incredible experiences over the past year. But this wasn't just about sharing a conversation or a moment—it was about something far greater. Sitting on that airplane, I knew I was meant to write all of this down and share this journey with as many people as possible.

Why?

So that I can offer hope to those who feel lost, show them that God is always present—even in the silence—and remind them that no matter where they are, their story matters too.

So that I can spread the Gospel, showing how His grace transforms even the most broken moments into something beautiful.

To tell this story to you, I first had to conquer my own fears, doubts, and insecurities before I could move to the next puzzle. It meant unpacking the boxes where I had buried all the moments I wanted to forget—the times I stumbled, the struggles I tried to hide—and laying them bare for the world to see. But through it all, God has shown me that vulnerability is not a weakness—it's a way to let His light shine through the cracks.

For me, this is just the beginning. God has ordered my steps—every single one—and now it's time to live fully in the purpose He has laid out for me.

My mission trip journal

PART SIX
EPILOGUE

Ephesians 2:8 "God saved you by his grace when you believed. And you can't take credit for this; it is a gift from God."

THE BEGINNING OF THE NEXT CHAPTER

Isaiah 6:8 *"Then I heard the Lord asking, "Whom should I send as a messenger to this people? Who will go for us?" I said, "Here I am. Send me."*

Since returning from El Salvador, my communication with God has become clearer, as if a channel is widening with each passing day. Looking back, I now see that writing this book was part of that journey. Each chapter unfolded naturally, and I began to recognize that I was simply telling the story He had already written.

It was surprisingly enjoyable—especially for a math major like me—because I wasn't bound by the constraints of plot twists or character development. I was simply recounting my own experiences, watching patterns emerge that I hadn't noticed before. Through the process, I realized I had been living in the pages of a story God had written long ago. And because He knew every single page and chapter, His timing was perfect.

While writing, I uncovered countless moments that once seemed insignificant but, in hindsight, were clearly orchestrated by divine timing.

RECAPPING WITH GINA

In September, I was talking with Gina to ensure I had accurately documented our conversations. During our chat, she mentioned that the only reason she brought up the Texas house was that she and Eleanor were such good friends. She felt comfortable enough to share that our dream house was spiritually corrupted—something she had never done with any other client.

As we talked about the "low vibrational entity" I reminded her that the same night I got off our Zoom call, I found City Point. She suddenly recalled that she was supposed to reach out to a friend who could help me with the "entity." Gina admitted she never acted on that because something told her it wasn't urgent. "I remember thinking, 'I'll get to it when I get to it,'" she said. "You know, thinking about it now, that doesn't make any sense. It's like going to a doctor, getting a cancer diagnosis, and then scheduling an appointment for six months later."

In that moment, we both realized that God needed her to get my attention so I would find City Point. He knew that supernatural interactions were necessary, whether it was hearing shocking things about our house or receiving words from Pappy. If Gina had connected me with her friend, I might never have thought to seek help at a church. It was not only God's will that I ended up at City Point; it was His perfect timing that allowed it to happen.

THE NUMBER 9

Last fall, while spending time with some friends from church, the number nine came up in conversation. A pastor shared how it is often linked to divine completeness and the fulfillment of God's promises. It represents the fruits of the Holy Spirit and the power of God's presence in our lives, serving as a reminder of spiritual growth and the journey toward wholeness—especially during times of trials and tribulations.

- Paul, in Galatians 5:22-23 lists nine fruits of the Spirit: love, joy, peace, patience, kindness, goodness, faithfulness, gentleness, and self-control.

- There are nine gifts of the Holy Spirit listed in 1 Corinthians 12: wisdom, knowledge, discerning of spirits, faith, miracles, healing, tongues, interpretation, and prophecy.
- The number nine is sometimes associated with the finality of judgment. For instance, in the Book of Revelation, there are nine specific judgments (the seven trumpets and two additional ones) leading up to the end times.
- The ninth hour is significant in the New Testament as a time of prayer (Acts 3:1) and the hour when Jesus died, symbolizing a time of repentance.
- Nine months is the typical gestation period for humans, which can symbolize new life and beginnings.

At the time, I filed that discussion away in my brain under "C" for "cool story." But when I got home that day and sat down to edit a few chapters in the book, I started noticing recurring themes in my life:

- I have had 9 different operational assignments as an E-2C Naval Flight Officer.
- Eleanor and I have made 9 moves together.
- It was 9 months from the day I started at the big bank until the day I was laid off, which marked the beginning of significant changes in my life.
- It was 9 months from the breakdown at my brother's wedding to when I walked into City Point Church…at 9:00 AM.
- Another 9-month interval passed from my first visit to City Point until the El Salvador trip.

And wouldn't you know it? Exactly nine months passed between El Salvador and the book's release. Completely unintentional—but it just happened that way.

What does that all mean? No idea, but it's pretty cool.

BIBLE VERSES

As I began writing in July, I noticed something remarkable—every day, without fail, scripture aligned perfectly with whatever chapter I was working on. Verses would appear in my Bible app or during daily readings, speaking directly to the themes in this book. Some days, I had three or four to choose from, and my list of unused verses kept growing.

On my final day of writing, I was still searching for the right verse to close the epilogue. That morning, I attended a prayer group at church, led by Pastor Stephen. As he began, he opened with Isaiah 6:8:

> *"Then I heard the Lord asking, 'Whom should I send as a messenger to this people? Who will go for us?' I said, 'Here I am. Send me.'"*

It was like a giant neon sign flashing right in front of me. On the very first day of this journey, Pastor Stephen answered my knock at the church door. Now, as I finished writing this book, he provided the exact verse I needed—though I have no doubt the Holy Spirit provided it through him.

And the verse hit me directly, because God has been using me as His messenger to people who are struggling and in need of hope. He continually places individuals in my life for reasons I don't always understand, but I say *"yes"* to His call, even when I don't know what the question is.

HEARING THE HOLY SPIRIT

Recently, my family went out to dinner at a Brazilian steakhouse with some friends. While I love all-you-can-eat steak, I wasn't looking forward to spending over $300 to feed my kids at a restaurant. But a tiny voice inside told me to just go along with it.

We were seated together in the bar area, and my friend's wife—who happens to be Brazilian—ordered off the menu for all of us. Our server seemed flustered throughout the night for reasons I'll never know. At the end of the evening, as she delivered our checks, two amazing things happened.

First, our check totaled $47.00. No idea how that happened—especially since Eleanor and I probably drank that much in wine alone. But God obviously knew I was concerned about money.

As we waited for the check, I felt the Holy Spirit nudge me to start a conversation. So, I casually asked our waitress, "Are you a Cowboys fan?"

"Oh, no," she replied. "I'm actually from South Carolina."

"Really? Where in South Carolina?" I asked.

"It's a really small town; you've probably never heard of it..."

"Is it Sumter?" A few years ago, I had taken a work team down for a two-week mission at Shaw Air Force Base, just a few minutes from the small town of Sumter. When my parents decided they wanted to retire and move south, Sumter was one of the towns they considered.

The look on her face was priceless. "How did you know?" she asked.

"Oh, I was just guessing," I replied.

She began to open up about her childhood in Sumter, sharing how a medical condition had affected her speech when she was younger. As she spoke, the Holy Spirit stirred something within me. I could see a picture form in my mind, and I felt that familiar heart squeeze—He was urging me to speak to her.

She described how her teachers and other kids all thought she was stupid, how she was constantly made fun of. She talked about finally receiving a diagnosis and how the treatment that followed changed her life.

We continued to chat for a few minutes, and as we were preparing to leave, she said "God bless you all, have a great night." That was the cue that I needed. I waited for the right moment to talk to her privately. As we were walking out, she was at the next table, cleaning up after another group.

I walked up to her and said, "It sounds like you're a believer, and I hope you're ok with me sharing this. I feel like God wants you to know that throughout your struggles, He was with you. He's proud of you—proud of everything you've accomplished since moving to Dallas—and He loves you. You shouldn't be embarrassed by your condition; instead, you should talk freely about your story so that others can learn from it."

She stared back at me for a few seconds, her face frozen.

Oh no, she's getting ready to call the cops.

Then her eyes filled with tears. "You have no idea what this means to me," she said. "I've been praying for a sign, and you just confirmed it."

Without another word, she embraced me like an old friend. As I walked away, I knew I had done exactly what God asked—nothing more, nothing less.

Moments like this have become more frequent as I've grown closer to God. But as much as I've learned to hear His voice, I've also gained a clearer understanding of the forces working against us.

In fact, the enemy isn't at all what I thought. He isn't the Hollywood villain, dressed in red with a pitchfork, spewing fire and brimstone. Instead, he is subtle, quiet, and cunning. He whispers lies into your heart—small, deceptive thoughts that feed fear, doubt, and shame, turning you away from God without you even realizing it.

On the flip side, the Holy Spirit is a gentle, loving presence. He is the quiet voice that reassures you, the small nudge that leads you back to the truth, and the constant reminder of God's love and the kingdom of heaven.

When you're not listening for God, the silence is easily filled by the enemy's lies—whispers of fear, doubt, and shame that pull you further from the truth. But when you're in tune with Him, God's voice breaks through, silencing those lies and speaking life, hope, and purpose into your soul. One thing is undeniable—God is always speaking. The real question is: Are we listening?

THE CAMARILLO HOUSE

For years, whenever we talked about our house in Camarillo, we believed the apparition Eleanor saw upstairs was real. But we never understood what it was or why it was there. While writing that chapter and revisiting our experiences in Camarillo, my hands froze over the keyboard as a vivid visualization filled my mind: an angel entering our home, bringing divine protection while I was away.

Wanting to capture that thought, I began jotting it down, but as I wrote, full-body chills swept over me, followed by the unmistakable warmth of heart-squeezing confirmation. I sat at my desk, tears of joy streaming down my face, finally realizing what had truly happened all those years ago.

Now, I have no doubt—there was an evil entity in that house, and God sent an angel to protect us.

WHAT DOES ALL THIS MEAN FOR YOU?

For weeks, I wrestled with how to conclude this book. This isn't a "5 Steps to Success" story. It's not a self-help manual, nor a novel with neatly wrapped-up endings. This is my testimony—an account of how God has worked in my life and spoken to me, even when I wasn't listening.

But, if there's one thing that I hope you take away from my story, it's the importance of having a relationship with God. Not just knowing about Him, memorizing bible verses, or going through the motions, but truly seeking Him, listening, and allowing Him to guide your life.

So, how do *you* hear Him? Let me share an example.

A few days before I finished this manuscript, I was out running an errand, driving alone in my truck, lost in thought. That week, I was having one of those "woe is me" moments. As I drove, I asked God a question out loud: *"Can you show me a time when you were with me, and I didn't realize it?"*

There was no audible voice that answered. No burning bush, no cloud or lightning, no dove descending from the heavens. Instead, a series of images started flashing through my mind, like snapshots in a half-finished video.

First came a memory of Jake and me, twelve years old, hands on the Ouija board, laughing as it moved under our fingers. And I could see God standing there in my living room, watching us with a look of disappointment, yet staying close to protect us.

Then came a vivid image from flight school in 1999, during an aircraft mishap in Pensacola, FL. I was in an orange-and-white-painted T-34 training aircraft with one of the instructors. After we landed and rolled down the runway, we paused on the taxiway, waiting for our wingman to land.

Suddenly, the nosewheel of our plane dropped into a sinkhole that had opened beneath us. The actual mishap probably lasted 12 seconds, but it felt like an eternity as the pilot and I quickly threw off the canopy and sprinted across the airfield to safety. In the replay of those moments, I once again saw God there, standing calmly in the grass between the runways, ensuring no one was harmed by the flying debris as the propellers struck the pavement and the engine came to a grinding halt.

Next, I saw myself on that nighttime mission in Afghanistan in 2002, when our right engine suddenly imploded while we were returning to the aircraft carrier. He took me back to that night, to the exact moment I saw the fireball as the engine tore itself apart mid-flight. God was with us, in the plane, guiding us back to the ship over miles of ocean and ensuring we landed safely.

Then I saw myself at my brother's wedding, leaving in the middle of the reception, trying to escape the demons in my head. He walked beside me across the grass, step-by-step, a Father watching over His son.

And He showed me that moment on the closet floor a few days later, curled up and alone in the dark, thoughts of suicide swirling through my mind. I watched Him walk into the closet with Eleanor, sit down beside her on the floor, and put His hand on my back right next to hers. As Eleanor whispered, "I'm here. It's OK," I saw his mouth move as He spoke the same words, perfectly in sync with my wife. And then, in that closet, He assured me that my next steps were already written, and they were going to be amazing.

The last image he showed me was of Him in the passenger seat of my truck, sitting beside me as I drove. It was like watching a live movie of myself, in real time. He looked over at me, then over at the steering wheel, as if reminding me that He was the one really in control. My hands were on a wheel that was just there for show.

I know some of you might be thinking, "What are you talking about? How do you know all this, and how does it help me?"

It's simpler than it sounds. Two years ago, I would have dismissed all these images as *"just my thoughts,"* like old memories resurfacing. But, I *asked* Him the question, and He answered me. And every single image, every half-finished video came with the same words that I saw clearly in my mind: *I Was With You.*

And through that entire conversation, which might have lasted 60 seconds, I felt that familiar squeeze in my heart, and the tears flowed like wine.

I didn't have to say anything back to Him, other than *"Thank you."*

It's that easy.

I'm not any different than you. I'm not special, I don't have any super-powers, I'm not a healer, I'm not a prophet. I'm just a dude, one of God's many children, just like you are.

He hears you, and He wants to talk to you. Ask Him a question, and then…listen. Really listen. And when you see that picture form in your head, recognize it for what it is: *His Voice.*

Don't wait. Seek him, right now. It will change your life.

WHAT'S NEXT FOR ME?

This journey has already been a success, even if the only copy of this book sits on my coffee table at home. It has sparked meaningful conversations, opened doors, and deepened my faith. For that, I am profoundly grateful.

And speaking of doors opening…

Right after I returned, an opportunity came up to enroll in a two-year ministry program through City Point and the Destiny Leadership Institute. I didn't hesitate to sign up. It's been one of the greatest learning opportunities in my life.

In August, I was presented with an opportunity to step up to a leadership position within the point teams at City Point, and I said "Yes" without hesitation.

Those are sentences I never imagined writing about myself.

Thank you for walking this path with me. I hope that somewhere in these pages, you found a piece of your story, a reflection of your own struggles, and perhaps, a glimpse of God's plan for you. Maybe you'll write a few sentences a year from now, and say "Man, didn't see that one coming." I've created a place for you to share your testimony with others—visit www.benduelley.com to find out how.

I don't know what's next. I don't know if I'll live to be 100 or if I might get hit by a bus tomorrow. But I do know that my journey is being written by a power far greater than my own.

For now, I'm listening for His voice. I'm waiting to see where the next path leads. I'm waiting to see what God will ask next. And whatever the question is, my answer is simple.

"Here I am. Send me."

ACKNOWLEDGMENTS

Above all, I want to thank God for guiding me through every moment of this journey. Even when I wasn't listening, You were always speaking, leading me toward light and hope. This book is a testament to Your grace, love, and faithfulness.

Throughout the writing process, I had countless conversations with friends, each contributing to the stories, thoughts, and memories within these pages. These discussions opened up deep and meaningful dialogues that shaped the content of this book. I want to acknowledge a few individuals: Jake Attanasio, Mike Feller, Paul "Pud" Dale, Steve "Wipe" Delanty, Pat "Chowdah" Haley, Jason "Suede" Pratt, Justin Puhl, Jeff Wicker, Benjie Esguerra, Brad Kaufman, Wayne Brinkman, Ty Rose, Travis "Poops" Overstreet, Mike "Verbal" Nunziato, Pastor Robert Garcia, and Marc Liebman.

To my great friend Peter Overland, who read this manuscript more times than I can count—your invaluable feedback at every turn has profoundly shaped this book, and I can't thank you enough.

Thanks to Pastor Stephen Tucker for not only answering my knock but also for walking with me on my spiritual journey. You've been a pastor, a guide, a counselor, and most importantly, a friend.

To Pastor Eddie & Pastor Julie, thank you for all that you do. It's incredible to reflect on the divine connections and paths that led my family to your doorstep.

To the pastors, synergy leads, point team leads, and the entire congregation at City Point Church—your role in my story has been profound, often in ways you may not even realize. Without the open doors my family and I walked through in 2023, I wouldn't be where I am today. The impact you've made on my life is immeasurable, and I'm forever grateful.

Gina, you've been a counselor, a healer, a friend, and so much more. God brought us together at exactly the right time, and through you, He accomplished something truly extraordinary in my life. And knowing that you were saved in 2024 makes it even more special.

To Pastor Wally Cook and the incredible team in El Salvador: God uses all of you to change lives, and I'm living proof. Raul, David, Marielos, you guys are amazing teachers, your devotion to the Lord is inspiring, and I can't wait to hang out with you all again and continue to learn.

I want to thank my mom, Cindy, and my dad, Jeff. Your love and support through all the different phases of my life have been amazing.

To my three incredible children—thank you for your love and strength, even though you didn't ask to be part of this journey with me. You kept me going through every challenge in my life.

And finally, to my loving wife, Eleanor, who has been by my side through it all, in the best and hardest of times. I love you more than words can express.

- October 2024.

BIBLE VERSES

The Bible is the only book ever written where the author is always present. – Unknown

Psalm 34:18 *"The Lord is close to the brokenhearted and saves those who are crushed in spirit."*

1 Peter 5:7 *"Give all your worries and cares to God, for he cares about you."*

John 1:1-4 *"In the beginning the Word already existed. The Word was with God, and the Word was God. He existed in the beginning with God. God created everything through him, and nothing was created except through him. The Word gave life to everything that was created, and his life brought light to everyone."*

Proverbs 16:9 *"We can make our plans, but the Lord determines our steps."*

Psalm 56:8 *"You keep track of all my sorrows. You have collected all my tears in your bottle. You have recorded each one in your book."*

1 Corinthians 9:24 *"Don't you realize that in a race everyone runs, but only one person gets the prize? So run to win!"*

1 Corinthians 15:10 *"But whatever I am now, it is all because God poured out his special favor on me—and not without results. For I have worked harder than any of the other apostles; yet it was not I but God who was working through me by his grace."*

Revelation 3:8 *"I know all the things you do, and I have opened a door for you that no one can close."*

Philippians 1:6 *"And I am certain that God, who began the good work within you, will continue his work until it is finally finished on the day when Christ Jesus returns."*

Genesis 2:18 *"Then the Lord God said, 'It is not good for the man to be alone. I will make a helper who is just right for him.'"*

Proverbs 16:1 *"We can make our own plans, but the Lord gives the right answer."*

Exodus 18:17-18 *"This is not good!" Moses' father-in-law exclaimed. "You're going to wear yourself out—and the people, too. This job is too heavy a burden for you to handle all by yourself."*

Mark 10:8-9 (NIV) *"…and the two will become one flesh. So they are no longer two, but one flesh. Therefore what God has joined together, let no one separate."*

Isaiah 43:16 *"I am the Lord, who opened a way through the waters, making a dry path through the sea."*

Philippians 2:13 *"For God is working in you, giving you the desire and the power to do what pleases him."*

Revelation 3:17 *"You say, 'I am rich. I have everything I want. I don't need a thing!' And you don't realize that you are wretched and miserable and poor and blind and naked."*

Ecclesiastes 3:1 *"For everything there is a season, a time for every activity under heaven."*

Proverbs 17:22 *"A cheerful heart is good medicine, but a broken spirit saps a person's strength."*

Proverbs 14:29 *"People with understanding control their anger; a hot temper shows great foolishness."*

Matthew 14:30-31 *"But when he saw the wind, he was afraid and, beginning to sink, cried out, 'Lord, save me!' Immediately Jesus reached out his hand and caught him. 'You of little faith,' he said, 'why did you doubt?'"*

Deuteronomy 31:8 *"Do not be afraid or discouraged, for the Lord will personally go ahead of you. He will be with you; he will neither fail you nor abandon you."*

Psalm 42:11 *"Why am I discouraged? Why is my heart so sad?"*

Ezekiel 37:5 *"This is what the Sovereign Lord says: Look! I am going to put breath into you and make you live again!"*

Psalm 31:9 *"Have mercy on me, Lord, for I am in distress. Tears blur my eyes. My body and soul are withering away."*

Galatians 6:2 *"Share each other's burdens, and in this way obey the law of Christ."*

Psalm 31:10 *"I am dying from grief; my years are shortened by sadness. Sin has drained my strength; I am wasting away from within."*

1 Peter 5:8-9 *"Stay alert! Watch out for your great enemy, the devil. He prowls around like a roaring lion, looking for someone to devour. Stand firm against him, and be strong in your faith. Remember that your family of believers all over the world is going through the same kind of suffering you are."*

Proverbs 20:5 *"The purposes of a person's heart are deep waters, but one who has insight draws them out."*

Matthew 7:24-25 *"Anyone who listens to my teaching and follows it is wise, like a person who builds a house on solid rock. Though the rain comes in torrents and the floodwaters rise and the winds beat against that house, it won't collapse because it is built on bedrock."*

Ecclesiastes 11:5 *"As you do not know what is the way of the wind, or how the bones grow in the womb of her who is with child, so you do not know the works of God who makes everything."*

Proverbs 3:33 (NIV) *"The Lord's curse is on the house of the wicked, but he blesses the home of the righteous."*

Jeremiah 30:17 *"I will give you back your health and heal your wounds,"* says the Lord.

Proverbs 17:6 *"Grandchildren are the crowning glory of the aged; parents are the pride of their children."*

Deuteronomy 18:10-11 *"…And do not let your people practice fortune-telling, or use sorcery, or interpret omens, or engage in witchcraft, or cast spells, or function as mediums or psychics, or call forth the spirits of the dead."*

Psalm 91:11 *"For he will order his angels to protect you wherever you go."*

Ephesians 6:12 *"For we are not fighting against flesh-and-blood enemies, but against evil rulers and authorities of the unseen world, against mighty powers in this dark world, and against evil spirits in the heavenly places."*

Job 33:14-15 *"For God speaks again and again, though people do not recognize it. He speaks in dreams, in visions of the night, when deep sleep falls on people as they lie in their beds."*

Luke 15:3-7 *"Then Jesus told them this parable: 'Suppose one of you has a hundred sheep and loses one of them. Doesn't he leave the ninety-nine in the open country and go after the lost sheep until he finds it? And when he finds it, he joyfully puts it on his shoulders and goes home. Then he calls his friends and neighbors together and says, 'Rejoice with me; I have found my lost sheep.''"*

Revelation 3:20 (NIV) *"Here I am! I stand at the door and knock. If anyone hears my voice and opens the door, I will come in and eat with that person, and they with me."*

Matthew 7:7 *"Ask, and it will be given to you; seek, and you will find; knock, and it will be opened to you."*

Romans 10:9 *"If you openly declare that Jesus is Lord and believe in your heart that God raised him from the dead, you will be saved."*

Acts 16:18 *"This went on day after day until Paul got so exasperated that he turned and said to the demon within her, 'I command you in the name of Jesus Christ to come out of her.' And instantly it left her."*

1 Kings 19:11-12 *"Go out and stand before me on the mountain," the Lord told him. And as Elijah stood there, the Lord passed by, and a mighty wind-*

storm hit the mountain. It was such a terrible blast that the rocks were torn loose, but the Lord was not in the wind. After the wind there was an earthquake, but the Lord was not in the earthquake. And after the earthquake there was a fire, but the Lord was not in the fire. And after the fire there was the sound of a gentle whisper.

Malachi 3:10 (NIV) *"Bring the whole tithe into the storehouse, that there may be food in my house. Test me in this," says the LORD Almighty, "and see if I will not throw open the floodgates of heaven and pour out so much blessing that there will not be room enough to store it."*

Isaiah 40:26 *"Lift up your eyes and look to the heavens: Who created all these? He who brings out the starry host one by one and calls forth each of them by name. Because of his great power and mighty strength, not one of them is missing."*

Matthew 28:19-20 *"Therefore, go and make disciples of all the nations, baptizing them in the name of the Father and the Son and the Holy Spirit. Teach these new disciples to obey all the commands I have given you. And be sure of this: I am with you always, even to the end of the age."*

Romans 12:2 *"Do not conform to the pattern of this world, but be transformed by the renewing of your mind. Then you will be able to test and approve what God's will is—his good, pleasing and perfect will."*

Acts 1:8 *"But you will receive power when the Holy Spirit comes upon you. And you will be my witnesses, telling people about me everywhere—in Jerusalem, throughout Judea, in Samaria, and to the ends of the earth."*

Proverbs 1:8-9 *"My child, listen when your father corrects you. Don't neglect your mother's instruction. What you learn from them will crown you with grace and be a chain of honor around your neck."*

John 10:27 *"My sheep hear my voice, and I know them, and they follow me."*

1 Corinthians 2:10 *"But it was to us that God revealed these things by his Spirit. For his Spirit searches out everything and shows us God's deep secrets."*

Acts 3:16 *"Through faith in the name of Jesus, this man was healed—and you* *know how crippled he was before. Faith in Jesus' name has healed him before your very eyes."*

Proverbs 4:22 *"For they bring life to those who find them, and healing to their whole body."*

Isaiah 58:10 *"Feed the hungry, and help those in trouble. Then your light will shine out from the darkness, and the darkness around you will be as bright as noon."*

Proverbs 22:6 *"Direct your children onto the right path, and when they are older, they will not leave it."*

1 Thessalonians 5:11 *"So encourage each other and build each other up, just as you are already doing."*

John 14:16–18 *"And I will ask the Father, and he will give you another Advocate, who will never leave you. He is the Holy Spirit, who leads into all truth. The world cannot receive him, because it isn't looking for him and doesn't recognize him. But you know him, because he lives with you now and later will be in you."*

Psalm 34:17 *"The LORD hears his people when they call to him for help. He rescues them from all their troubles."*

Matthew 6:26 *"Look at the birds. They don't plant or harvest or store food in barns, for your heavenly Father feeds them. And aren't you far more valuable to him than they are?"*

Ephesians 6:10 *"Therefore, put on every piece of God's armor so you will be able to resist the enemy in the time of evil. Then after the battle you will still be standing firm."*

Ephesians 2:10 *"For we are God's masterpiece. He has created us anew in Christ Jesus, so we can do the good things he planned for us long ago."*

Psalm 107:28-29 *"'Lord, help!'" they cried in their trouble, and he saved them from their distress. He calmed the storm to a whisper and stilled the waves."*

Psalm 139:16 *"You saw me before I was born. Every day of my life was* recorded in your book. Every moment was laid out before a single day had passed."

Ephesians 2:8 *"God saved you by his grace when you believed. And you can't take credit for this; it is a gift from God."*

Isaiah 6:8 *"Then I heard the Lord asking, "Whom should I send as a messenger to this people? Who will go for us?" I said, "Here I am. Send me."*

ENDNOTES

2. FOUNDATIONS OF SUCCESS

1. Graduates are also eligible to request commissions in other services, though it is rare.

4. BUILDING ON THE FOUNDATIONS

1. Tecumseh Court (or T-Court) is now referred to as Tamanend's Court after the figurehead that has sat at the entrance to Bancroft Hall since the Civil War. https://www.usna.edu/PAO/faq_pages/Tamanend.php

5. SUCK IT UP, BUTTERCUP

1. My callsign in the Navy was actually Boo Boo, but it had nothing to do with that kind of booboo. Ask me the story if we're ever out at a bar together.

6. LIFE AS A MIDSHIPMAN

1. If you don't know who 2 Live Crew is, they were a hip hop group that was popular in the late 80s & early 90s. Don't play any of their songs without headphones in. And definitely don't search for them online if you're at work.
2. Read more about Naval Air Station Pensacola at Commander, Navy Region Southwest website: https://cnrse.cnic.navy.mil/Installations/NAS-Pensacola/About/, retrieved August 12, 2024.

7. TAKING FLIGHT

1. Military One Source, https://installations.militaryonesource.mil/military-installation/naval-air-station-pensacola, retrieved August 12, 2024.
2. The flight training path has changed over the years. The current training pipeline can be found on the Chief of Naval Air Training homepage https://www.cnatra.navy.mil/training-nfo.asp.
3. The F-14 Tomcat was officially retired in September 2006, replaced by the F/A-18 Super Hornet. In 2009, the first EA-6B Prowler squadron transitioned to the F/A-18G Growler, and the Prowler was officially retired in 2015. Most NFOs were able to make the transition to the new platforms, but others were sent to different communities. The E-2 Hawkeye is still in production to this day, and as it turned out, the E-2 path was the best thing that could have ever happened in my career. God's hand steered my journey, and His plans were woven into the fabric of my flight suit experiences, leading me exactly where I needed to be so that he could use me later. But, I just didn't know it at the time.

8. A CHANCE ENCOUNTER

1. ROTC stands for Reserve Officers' Training Corps, which are university-based training programs for commissioned officers.

9. THINGS CHANGE

1. Though these are not "actual" conversations between me and the United States Navy, they are pretty dang close, and represent back and forth emails & phone calls that were happening with my Detailers over the years. Community Detailers are the military officers who work in Millington, TN at the Navy Personnel Command. Their role is to work with you to fill available jobs for follow-on assignments, trying to match your career interests with the needs of the Navy. They are studs, and most times their jobs are thankless.
2. A few days after 9/11, I wrote down everything that I could remember about that day in a notebook. That journal has long been tossed in the trash, but I still have my flight logbook from that day. Timeline of the events retrieved from https://miller center.org/remembering-september-11/september-11-terrorist-attacks, and the History Channel talks about the order from the White House: https://www.history. com/news/september-11-attacks-shootdown-order-cheney-bush

13. FIRST CHOICE!

1. Both Eleanor and I heard the nurse say "blah blah Mädchen blah blah hier." If you actually speak German, you don't have to call me out and say "That's not how a German would say it!" I took the liberty to use Google and filled in the "blahs".

20. THE PRESSURE CHAMBER

1. And yes, I convinced Eleanor to choose the name Tyler for our first child, but didn't tell her why until much, much later.

27. GINA DOES WHAT?

1. Yes, I know about the whole *Hitchhiker's Guide to the Galaxy* thing.
2. Read more about Dr. Nelson and Emotion Code at https://drbradleynelson.com/

34. HOW GOD SPEAKS TO YOU

1. Don't worry, I'm not giving away the real answers to escape rooms. That would be low class.

40. SHOW ME THE MONEY!

1. I don't want to give the impression that I have stacks of cash sitting around my house in a safe. Nothing could be further from the truth.

42. INTRO TO WALLY

1. Listen to Pastor Wally's message here https://citypointchurch.subspla.sh/zp4h6td.

43. HEADED SOUTH

1. It's a great read! https://www.amazinglovemissions.com/e-books/

45. UNDERSTAND GOD'S GIFTS

1. Yes, I looked it up. https://www.worldatlas.com/animals/how-many-legs-does-a-spider-have.html#:
2. I tried to recall this from memory, and actually got pretty close https://www.med.-navy.mil.

46. I DON'T KNOW ... BLUE?

1. https://www.amazinglovemissions.com/wp-content/uploads/2015/11/HealingIs Easy_WallyCook.pdf, Chapter 9. Retrieved September 28th, 2024.

55. SPIRITUAL WARFARE IN SAN MARTIN

1. That's a nicer version of what I actually said.

ABOUT THE AUTHOR

CAPTAIN BEN DUELLEY, USN (Ret) is a decorated combat veteran with over 24 years of distinguished military service. He has deployed seven times across the globe, supporting operations in the Middle East, Pacific Theater, Africa, and South America.

Ben was the Commanding Officer of the VAW-113 Black Eagles, served as the Flag Aide to the Deputy Assistant Secretary of the Navy for International Programs, and spent time in the Pentagon managing large-scale budgets and aviation requirements. Throughout his career he had the privilege of serving alongside thousands of sailors, an experience that shaped him in ways he never expected.

Ben holds a Bachelor of Science in Mathematics from the United States Naval Academy and a Master's in National Strategic Studies from the Naval War College. He is currently studying at City Point College and the Destiny Leadership Institute, pursuing ordination as a pastor.

His debut book, *God Was Always Speaking, I Just Wasn't Listening*, shares his story of facing internal battles, discovering God's presence, and finding new direction in serving others.

He resides in Texas with his wife, Eleanor, and their three children.

www.benduelley.com

facebook.com/benduelleyauthor
linkedin.com/in/ben-duelley